T0120784

BREAK OUT
and
BREAK FORTH

Maximise Your God-Given Gifts

DR ROBERT CANN

WestBow
PRESS®
A DIVISION OF THOMAS NELSON
& ZONDERVAN

WestBow Press books may be ordered through booksellers or by contacting:

WestBow Press
A Division of Thomas Nelson & Zondervan
1663 Liberty Drive
Bloomington, IN 47403
www.westbowpress.com
844-714-3454

ISBN: 978-1-6642-1847-5 (sc)
ISBN: 978-1-6642-1846-8 (hc)
ISBN: 978-1-6642-1848-2 (e)

Library of Congress Control Number: 2021903280

Print information available on the last page.

WestBow Press rev. date: 02/18/2021

I dedicate this book to my wife, Baaba Cann, and my three wonderful kids, Jerome, Jaidene, and Jaisen. I am grateful to you for being my rock and motivation. Your faithfulness, love, and dedication have seen me through the most difficult seasons of our life. Thank you for believing in me, for always being there, and for enriching and sharing my life. You are all special.

Break up your fallow ground.
—Jeremiah 4:3 (KJV)

Contents

Acknowledgements

I am grateful to the Almighty God for being my source of strength and hope. I feel humbled to be used as a vessel to reach out to the Body of Christ.

To my parents, David and Mary Cann, and my siblings. Thank you for your nurturing, love, guidance, counsel, and support all my years. You are deeply appreciated.

To Dag Heward-Mills, founder and presiding bishop of United Denomination of Lighthouse Group of Churches (UDOLGOC): thank you for providing spiritual covering over my life. I am grateful for instructions in wisdom, training in leadership, and the opportunity to pastor.

To Bishop EAT Sackey, you have been a big brother to me since I met you. Thank you for always being an example to me and for years of guidance and counsel. The Lord placed you in my life for a reason.

To Richard Aryee, the bishop of First Love Church, United Kingdom (UDOLGOC): you believed in me when others did not and gave me every opportunity to work in the vineyard of the Lord. You have been a source of strength and a pillar in my life. Thank you.

To my great friends Felix Manteaw, Barry Gyamfi and Alfred Sam, thank you for many years of amazing friendship, encouragement, and support. You have been more than brothers.

To the late Mr Ransford Brefo and his wife, Mrs Dorothy Brefo, and their family: you took me in as part of your family at a challenging period in my life. Your love and support sustained me in my night season. I will be eternally grateful.

To my uncle Joe Cann (Ghana), who raised and nurtured me from a very tender age, I thank you for my foundations in Christ, godly discipline, and teaching me how to read and write. I have become the man I am because of the foundations you provided me. May the Lord be gracious to you always.

Finally, to all who have been part of my life along life's journey: you have played no small part in making me the man I have become. I dedicate my very first book to you all. Thank you.

Introduction

My journey in life has been what I describe as exciting, interesting, and full of many challenges that life could throw at a person. However, at this juncture of my life, I have come to appreciate how God works to order our steps. (Job 23:9,10 – KJV)

I graduated as medical practitioner in 1997 with the Bachelor of Medicine and Bachelor of Surgery degrees as we call it and have been a full-time medical practitioner since then. I have also been serving in the ministry of our Lord Jesus Christ since I became born-again in 1996 and have been involved in teaching the word of God since then. I have also been involved in guidance and counselling for more than 20 years now. I have been blessed and privileged to have been trained, nurtured, and guided by seasoned ministers of the gospel. It is from this background that I share my experiences with anyone, who like myself, seeks to fulfil their God-given purpose in life.

Genesis 1: 28 says: "And God blessed them, and God said unto them, be fruitful and multiply and replenish the earth, and subdue it: and have dominion over the fish of the sea, and over the fowl of the air, and over every living thing that moveth upon the earth" (KJV)

God desires that we fulfil the potential that was placed in us at birth. He made us in his image, and if God is creative, it implies that man is designed to be creative.

To quote Shakespeare's *Twelfth Night*: "Be not afraid of greatness. Some are born great, some achieve greatness, and others have greatness thrust upon them".

Success has been defined in many ways. Dictionary.com offers definitions of success as "the attainment of wealth, position, honours, or the like" and "a person or thing that has had success, as measured by attainment of goals, wealth".

In the world in which we live today, a successful person is more likely to be defined by the attainment of wealth, position, power, and status rather than an attainment of one's goals. However, I believe that if a person can fulfil his or her God-given potential, discover the purpose for which he or she was created, and attain the goals a person wants to achieve, then he or she will have been a success. The attainment of such goals may not necessarily be accompanied by wealth, status, or power but if they achieve that purpose, they must be deemed successful.

Nelson Mandela once said, "What counts in life is not the mere fact that we have lived. It is what difference we have made to the lives of others that will determine the significance of the life we lead". That sums up successful living: affecting the lives of others in a positive way.

I believe real success and fulfilment in life is not determined by how rich one is. There is no set definition or criteria for success. Jesus made this clear. In Luke 12: 15 (KJV), Jesus said, "take heed, and beware of covetousness: for a man's life consisteth not in the abundance of the things which he possesseth".

I was born into what is called a working-class home, and on my journey through life, I have lived and experienced life in villages, small towns, and big cities. I have interacted with many people from all walks of life—different social classes, backgrounds, and cultures, some rich and some poor. During this time I have made some observations about successful people that I want to share with you in this book. These observations are by no means all there is to make one successful, but time and again it influenced whether a person achieved his or her life goals.

Except for a privileged few who are born with greatness thrust upon them, many great men and women rose from very humble beginnings to greatness.

Wilferd Arlan Peterson, an American author who wrote for This

Week magazine for many years, writes, "Great men are little men expanded; great lives are ordinary lives intensified". This means the extraordinary people you see or hear about were once ordinary people like you and me but have gone through a certain process or lifestyle change to become who they are today.

James 5: 17 encourages us: "Elijah was a man with a nature like ours [with the same physical, mental, and spiritual limitations and shortcomings], and he prayed intensely for it not to rain, and it did not rain on the earth for three years and six months" (Amplified Bible).

Simply put, Elijah was as human as we are, and if he could pray for such supernatural manifestations then we can do the same.

It appears some people are born with a gift or natural ability at doing something much more easily than others. But it goes without argument that most great people learnt or trained themselves to become great. Few are born with any special skills or abilities. You can also fulfil your potential and succeed despite your perceived disadvantages. Irrespective of where you were born, what family you were born into, your educational background, and where you grew up, you can turn your life around if you have the desire. And this is the key—a personal desire to succeed—because no one can wish that for you.

This book was borne out of a personal desire to encourage young people who have the potential to do well but have stuttered along the way. It is meant to encourage anyone who seeks inspiration to fulfil their God-given potential. There are many such books written about this subject by great men and women who have been a blessing to the body of Christ. However, I believe there is safety in the multitude of counsel.

God also uses different personalities to reach out to different groups, and I pray that you will find some words of wisdom in this book to ignite your passion. I hope it will enrich your life.

I also hope you will learn a few lessons that will add to the knowledge you already have and help you unlock your potential and break your fallow grounds. I hope it becomes a lifetime resource for you.

May you find encouragement to attain the victories you desire and inspiration as you read. May you receive divine wisdom to turn your life around to break out and break forth.

1

Created for a Purpose— Engineered for Greatness

> And God blessed them, and God said unto them, be fruitful, and multiply, and replenish the earth, and subdue it: and have dominion over the fish of the sea, and over the fowl of the air, and over every living thing that moveth upon the earth.

—Genesis 1: 28 (KJV)

Every human being is unique and born to accomplish a purpose. Irrespective of where you were born or the circumstances of your birth, you must understand that there is a potential in you for great accomplishments. You may feel disadvantaged in your present state, but if you are determined and believe in who God created you to be, you can turn your life around.

If you think about who you are, what you are, and what you can do, you will realise that you are different from everyone else. There are things you can do that others cannot. Every person is unique, but this potential is affected by various factors. When God created humans, he programmed and engineered us to be fruitful (Genesis 1: 28, 9: 1, 7, 48: 4).

Break out of Your Fallow Ground

So why are many of us not fulfilling our God-given potential? What prevents many a talented individual from getting to the very top in his or her chosen careers, business, or in ministry? For many of us, our untapped or unused talents or gifts are like fallow grounds.

What Is Fallow Ground?

The Oxford English Dictionary defines *fallow ground* as "farmland ploughed and harrowed but left for a period without being sown.... characterized by inaction and unproductive; when nothing seems to happen".

For many of us, our lives and talents have lain dormant for a long time without productivity or meaning, full of frustration. We know we should be better than we are now, and we are frustrated that we are not making progress despite the potential we may have. Our real potential lies unfulfilled and locked up. Like a padlock, it requires a specific key or solution to open it.

"For thus saith the Lord to the Men of Judah and Jerusalem, Break up your fallow ground, and sow not among thorns" (Jeremiah 4: 3).

The Strong's Concordance refers to *fallow ground* as untilled or tillable ground. It is land that is tillable but remains untilled. Therefore, that land is not yielding anything because it has not been broken up so that seeds can be planted.

According to the Matthew Henry Concise Commentary on the Whole Bible 16623, fallow ground is "ground capable of improvement; it is our ground, let out to us, and we must be accountable for it; but it is fallow; it is unfenced and lies common; it is unfruitful and of no advantage to the owner".

The following scripture is essentially referencing an unrepentant heart that must change to receive mercy from God; a fallow ground can also be translated to mean unused talent or a gift that must be used to bring benefits to the owner of that ground. "He who cultivates his land will have plenty of bread, but he who follows worthless people and frivolous pursuits will have plenty of poverty" (Proverbs 28: 19 Amplified Bible).

This scripture clearly describes working with your gifts or talents and using the resources God has given you. Literally anyone who does not use his or her God-given gifts or talent will be doomed to an ordinary life and will exist without fulfilment. It means you must use the gifts God has given you or improve on the gifts God has blessed you with to be rewarded.

Africa is a prime example of a continent that does not 'till its land', and it is obvious that 'it has poverty enough'. The land of Africa is blessed with resources: gold, diamond, bauxite, oil, uranium, and many other rich minerals. In addition, most of Africa has rich, arable land that, with utilisation of modern technology and knowledge, can be tilled for our benefit. The great majority of Africans are very industrious and entrepreneurial, and certainly in modern times we have been blessed with intellectuals who are excelling in the diaspora. Why then is Africa deemed poor and classified as a third-world continent? Why should the inhabitants of a continent so blessed with natural resources live in dire poverty?

Anyone who makes the effort to use their God-given gifts, talents, or resources will, in a matter of time, excel. This is the 'value-added life'— the more you process or enhance your gifts, the better your life becomes.

God's original vision was for humanity to be fruitful and victorious. He blessed humanity and decreed that it should flourish. In simple terms, we must "wax great, and go forward, and grow until we become very great" (Genesis 26: 13). God does not desire that we should live a life of poverty and daily struggles. When the child of God lives a life of abject poverty, full of struggles and frustrations, it implies that either God is not real or that his word is not true. But we know that God is not a liar and that he watches over his word to perform it. Many of us do not have faith enough. We limit God and, in many cases, even doubt if he will fulfil his word concerning us.

In 2 Kings 4: 1–6 (English Standard Version), the prophet Elisha asked the widow of the deceased prophet to "go outside, borrow vessels from all your neighbours, empty vessels and not a few". Elisha wanted her to trust God for an unlimited breakthrough.

The poor widow did not understand the principle of the limitless blessings that I believe God desires to shower upon his faithful ones. She borrowed only a few vessels and filled until "the oil stopped flowing". I believe the oil would have continued to flow if she had more empty vessels available. She had placed limits on the power of God and possibly did not have much faith in the words of the prophet. She had small expectations and could have trusted God more.

God has declared in his precious Word: "A man's gift makes room for him and brings him before the great" (Proverbs 18: 16 ESV). It is your gift that is meant to bring you success or promotion (making room for you).

Principles for Success

There are principles by which success can be achieved, and they will work whether you practice them in Aberdeen or in Zulutown. It is important to understand that education and training are important, but success does not only depend on having a high IQ (Ecclesiastes 9: 11).

It is also important to understand that whilst prayer and reading the Word of God are key cornerstones for successful Christian living, there is also a place for using your mind to reason and to apply the wisdom God has given you through his Word. You can be highly educated and be poor, just as you can be illiterate and be a millionaire. You can find highly educated Christians who are poor, just as you will find uneducated Christians who are extremely rich.

"I have seen servants upon horses, and princes walking as servants upon the earth" (Ecclesiastes 10: 7).

Ecclesiastes 9: 11 (ESV) makes us understand that "under the sun the race is not to the swift, nor the battle to the strong, nor bread to the wise, nor riches to the intelligent, nor favour to those with knowledge, but time and chance happen to them all".

Solomon makes an interesting observation—he saw people who were not necessarily endowed with skill or knowledge becoming more successful than those who were. We can, therefore, conclude that there are factors other than your talents that greatly influence whether you succeed or fail in life.

I have come to appreciate that you can succeed if you are willing to apply the principles of success and pay the price to achieve it. Break the principles, and they will break you; use them well, and they will help you succeed.

Just as a tasty recipe is a combination of the ingredients and process of cooking, so does success depend on many factors. Some of the major principles of success are obvious, as we all know, but there are also minor factors that can, more than anything else, be the difference between being successful and failing spectacularly. These can be likened to what the bible calls "the little foxes that spoil the vine" Song of Songs 2:15 (KJV). Foxes are very clever animals; they operate with subtlety and would usually destroy the grapes in a vine before they are ripe. They prevent the grapes from reaching harvest. In the same way unseemly 'little' character flaws can prevent you from reaching your full potential.

Not every successful person was born with a silver spoon in his or her mouth. There are many rags-to-riches stories to fill us with hope. Reading about many successful people has taught me that most of them came from humble beginnings, like you and me.

The great scientist Sir Isaac Newton was not born into a rich family. His father was a farmer who died before Isaac was born. He was already disadvantaged when he was born. Newton was not the cleverest pupil in class when he attended Grantham Grammar School and was described as bottom of the class in every subject. Newton however did not use his limitations as an excuse not to excel. He eventually rose to become one of the greatest scientists this world was blessed with. If he could, so can you. I see you moving forward and doing well in Jesus's name.

2

What Is in Your Hand?

> "The Lord said to him, what is that in your hand? He
> said, a staff. And he said, throw it on the ground. So
> he threw it on the ground, and it became a serpent,
> and Moses ran from it". And thou shalt take this rod
> in thine hand, wherewith thou shalt do signs.
>
> —Exodus 4: 2, 17 (ESV)

I believe God has already equipped us with talents enough for us to excel and grace to harness our talents. Let's review.

Following the scripture above the title, we add, "And thou shalt take this rod in thine hand, wherewith thou shalt do signs" (Exodus 4: 17 ESV).

In chapter 3–4, God tried to send Moses to accomplish an assignment, but Moses tried to find every excuse why he was not up to the task. He felt incapable and inadequately equipped to accomplish it. It looked impossible. He initially gave the excuse that he was 'a nobody' and then later stated that the Israelites would not believe him. His last excuse was that he was not eloquent enough and was not a good public speaker. With every excuse, God gave him a solution and tried to prove to him that as far as he was concerned, Moses was well equipped and able to accomplish what God wanted him to do. The impossible is possible with God, and he was trying to tell Moses that he was the source of all sufficiency. The Lord said unto him, Who hath made man's mouth? Or who maketh the dumb, or deaf, or seeing, or the blind? Have not I the Lord?" – Exodus 4:11, KJV

Jehovah was trying to impress upon Moses that He created man and equipped him to accomplish things. Sometimes we look at ourselves and wonder if any good could come out of us. Many of us do not believe that seeds of greatness have already been sown in us. We live in doubt, never believing we are capable of any accomplishments. If only you can believe in yourself and take one small step at a time, that seed which is already in you will blossom when the time and conditions are right.

"And she said, as the Lord thy God liveth, I have not a cake, but an handful of meal in a barrel, and a little oil in a cruse: and, behold, I am gathering two sticks, that I may go in and dress it for me and my son, that we may eat it, and die" (1 Kings 17: 12).

In the time of famine and great difficulty, the widow at Zarephath could not appreciate that God had made provision for her to sustain her through the famine. She lacked an understanding about the value of what she had. Her encounter with Elijah transformed what she saw as insignificant into something significant that saved an entire family.

"Elisha said to her, 'What can I do for you? Tell me, what do you have in your house?' She answered, 'Your servant has nothing in the house except a small jar of olive oil'" (2 Kings 4: 2 New English Translation). The prophet's widow lamented that she had nothing when she had a jar of oil. She just lacked the understanding of what could be accomplished with that small jar. To her it was insignificant, and in her mind she had no gift, treasure, or opportunity. Oil represents the power and presence of God, and the Holy Spirit in a sense. In the case of both widows, God made something available to work with.

The scriptures demonstrate two things: that God gives each of us something (a rod, a handful of meal, a cruse or jar of oil) to work with, and the grace (the divine ability) to harness that gift.

The 'rod in your hand' is what you will need 'to do signs'. The 'handful of meal and little oil in a cruse' is what is meant to sustain you through a lifetime. The 'small jar of olive oil' is what you need to succeed. As insignificant as what your gifts may be to you, believe that in God's hands you can become great (Jeremiah 18: 3–6).

Your gift is what you need to make it in life. Your gift is what 'makes room' for you. It is your talent that can bring about your promotion and can usher you into greatness.

If used, your gift may even save you from poverty, financial hardship, or any frustrations you are facing right now. Both Elijah and Elisha made the widows aware of the unlimited potential they possessed and what could be accomplished if harnessed. Do not despite your gifts however small or insignificant they look. What you need is faith and to believe that if you persevere, it will eventually come good.

Every one of us is born with an innate talent, the seeds of greatness, and the raw materials required to being fruitful. What happens to that seed, gift, or talent depends on so many factors. For many years, this innate potential may lay unfulfilled, just like the potential that is within a bean seed or a grain of corn. That seed is like the oak within the acorn or the tree inside the mustard seed. If nobody can predict that a grain of corn could yield many ears of corn, then you can also not predict what your future would be. You must understand that God has placed a unique gift that you must maximise to become successful in life. It is all about discovering who you are and what you are good at and then maximising these talents.

A *rod* in Moses's hands became a snake; a *handful of meal and a little oil* in a cruse could feed a family for years; a *small jar of olive oil* paid off a family's debts; and two fishes and five loaves in Jesus's hands fed five thousand people (with a surplus of twelve baskets). What is in your hand may be small, but remember, even if your beginning was insignificant, your latter end can greatly increase (Job 8: 7).

God Gives Each of Us a Talent or Ability

"And unto one he gave five talents, to another two, and to another one; every man according to their several ability; and straightway took his journey. Then he that hath received the five talents went and traded with the same, and made them other five talents. And likewise he that had received two, he also gained other two. But he that had received one went and digged in the earth, and hid his lord's money" (Matthew 25: 15–18).

In his kindness, God gives every one of us a talent. Each gift comes packaged with its own special grace to allow it to flourish. A gift must be used by the individual for his or her own personal blessing as well as for the benefit of mankind. The gift or gifts should be continually developed for them to yield the desired blessing for the recipient. Failure to use the gifts may lead to a life of frustration and poverty.

When you buy new equipment—a car, television, an iPad, or any gadget—it comes with a manual explaining how to operate it to its maximum benefit. Everything necessary is built within that equipment. The inability to utilise the full benefits is not because the benefits do not exist but because of the ignorance of the user.

When God created you, He equipped you with all that is required to maximise your potential. Each seed or potential comes with own its own *grace* and *capacity* to maximise that potential. Inside that seed or gift there is provision, protection, and prosperity. Even with the same talents, people excel in different ways, because in each person, God gives a different grace (such as their strengths, capacities, and opportunities) to maximise those gifts. This means that you can accomplish what you must do effortlessly using your God-given talents.

"And he called his ten servants, and delivered them ten pounds, and said unto them, occupy till I come" (Luke 19: 13 King James Version). In this scripture, the nobleman gives a pound each to ten servants and asks them to work with it until a time when he would ask them to account for what they did with their gifts. The nobleman was fair and just because he gave everyone something to work with, a gift unique to them, and expected them to do something with it. Some utilised what was given to them, but one managed to find excuses why he did not use his gift. Upon his return, the nobleman was furious about the gift that was wasted. I find that interesting because many of us would have shrugged at that lazy servant and said, "Well, just leave him to rot". Not so with the nobleman. He punished the lazy man.

What you do with a seed or a talent is so important. You can either trade with it for it to be a blessing or you can hide it and never use it.

Many years ago, in Ghana, West Africa, there was a man called Tetteh Quarshie. In 1870 he travelled to an island in Equatorial Guinea called Fernando Po (now called Bioko). He stayed there for about six years and discovered cocoa beans. Tetteh Quarshie had several options what to do with the cocoa beans. He could have roasted and eaten the few cocoa beans he took from Fernando Po. But he was not selfish. He recognised the potential in those few cocoa beans. Unlike many of us he had the perception that those small beans had the potential to make a nation rich. He brought several cocoa beans back to Ghana and cultivated them. Other farmers soon planted the beans, and within a few years cocoa became a cash crop for a whole nation. Before 1980, Ghana was the largest exporter of cocoa, and to date, our cocoa remains one of the finest in the world.

Develop and Add Value to the Gift

Matthew 25: 15 teaches that God gives every one of us a talent according to our several abilities. This talent is meant to be utilised to bring a blessing to the individual and to benefit humankind. The more they traded with the talents, the more they gained. The worth of that talent increased—value added—as they continued to use it. Sometimes you may find yourself in a church, and your pastor may ask you to take up a role, such as ushering, playing the keyboard, singing, teaching Sunday school or a small group, or even helping to organise programmes. Each of these roles may appear insignificant to you, but that role is part of the process to help you develop that gift. When Joseph served as a steward in Potiphar's house (Genesis 39: 4, 6) as well as an overseer in prison (Genesis 39: 23–24), little did he know he was being prepared to serve as a steward in a greater capacity—as prime minister of Egypt.

I need you to understand that during your developmental stages, every assignment you are given has the potential to make you better. In a way, that role becomes your 'practising field or your wilderness' where you hone your skills to perfection. Joseph's skills at managing resources were perfected in Potiphar's house and in prison whilst David kept practising his harp in the wilderness until he became 'a cunning player on the harp' (1 Samuel 16–18). David used a sling and stones for many years as a shepherd. He strongly believed that small stones, capable of killing a bird, could also kill a giant.

The next time you have any opportunity to use your talents, be quick in seizing that opportunity, whether paid or unpaid.

Different gifts are given to everyone. For example, I can neither fly a plane nor be a scaffolder because I am not a great lover of heights, but I can read volumes of material without getting bored. You can stick me in a library full of books from morning until evening and I still would not get bored because I will always find something exciting to read each time. I observed workmen working on the Shard in London, and just gazing at their skill filled me with awe and admiration and an appreciation of God's wisdom and grace.

Some of us despise ourselves and fail to see how unique we are to others. As Paul explained in 1 Corinthians 23–26, God gives diverse gifts because the whole body cannot be an eye or an ear (everyone cannot be the same, no variety or diversity). It certainly would be a boring world without diversity. The different ethnicities, shapes, heights, weights, talents, and abilities are all beautifully created and work in harmony to fulfil God's divine purpose. This diversity and differences are so important to God that He instructed Noah to preserve in the ark two of a kind of every animal He had created.

You must appreciate who you are, your role in the body of

Christ, and how you work for the Lord with pride, knowing that God appreciates who you are and the contributions you are making to the body of Christ. Start using your gifts.

A Life-Changing Encounter

In September 2008 I had an amazing encounter with a patient in clinic. After the consultation, she asked whether I was a mentor or life coach. I said no. She said, "Dr Cann, I think you should be a life coach and mentor". I asked why she thought I could be either. Her response was, "I can see that you have a genuine interest in people and think you would be an excellent mentor".

I have never thought of myself as a mentor or life coach and I still do not feel so. What this lady and many others have said to me over the years made me aware of a potential gift I was not aware existed within me—the ability to reach out in a compassionate manner.

After this encounter, I thought about her statement and similar remarks a few others had made. It caused me to ponder whether this was a gift God had endowed me with.

When God called Samuel, he could not tell that it was the voice of God. God used Eli's voice to point Samuel in the direction of his calling. I believe Samuel knew Eli's unmistaken voice. After all, he had lived with Eli for more than ten years since he was born. He could not have been confused. I believe the lesson God wanted to teach Samuel was that even though he had been predestined to be the first prophet of Israel, he needed someone to point him in the right direction. He still needed a mentor or somebody to guide him to his destiny. The gift was there, the grace had been made available, but it required an experienced person to identify it and help him fulfil that gift. Samuel needed an 'Eli' just as all of us have needed mentors along life's highways. A lot of great people you read about were 'discovered' by others.

Many people have accidentally discovered what they were good at, often after their pastor, teacher, coach, trainer, father, guardian, or someone brought it to their attention. Do not take for granted the positive things people say about you. It may be that a hidden gift or talent is being unearthed.

An Avid Reader

My love for reading and writing began at a tender age. Reading came naturally. My uncle is a medical practitioner, and as a child, I visited him a few times in Accra, Ghana. In his house is a large study and a big library fully stocked with medical books. I spent most of the time reading his medical books with all those fascinating illustrations. My desire to become a medical doctor was first borne in that library, and my fascination with his medical books inspired me. Sometimes I went to the Kotoka International Airport with my cousin, who loved planes, just to watch them take off and land. We spent some time in a few flight simulators, but I never took to flying because it never stimulated me. My desire for reading volumes of material would form the basics of a life in the medical field. My cousin went on to become a pilot and still flies aircrafts.

I am trying to tell you, dear reader, that if you find yourself doing certain things, chances are you may be gifted in that area. We usually discover our gifts in the things that come naturally to us, things we find ourselves doing effortlessly and enjoy doing so well.

The Gift Is Present but Dormant: the Palm Tree inside the Kernel and the Oak in the Acorn

Inside every human being is potential and an innate gift or talent. The potential for the harvest is already lying dormant within the seed, and until the seed is exposed to the *conditions required* to make it develop, it will remain just an ordinary seed. This means that the gifts you have inside you will remain untapped or unused until it is placed in the *right* soil (environment) with the right conditions for growth. The palm kernel and acorn and mustard seeds are small, but the trees that grow from them are massive. You cannot tell the future potential of a person by looking at the beginnings or present circumstance.

Let me give you an illustration. If I place a grain of corn on a plate and store it in a safe place for many years, I will still only have one grain. If I take that same grain and place it in the right soil with the right conditions, within a year I will be guaranteed a harvest.

A few years ago, I watched a kids' movie called *A Bug's Life*. In one scene the main character, an ant called Flik, had a chat with another young ant. As they walked along a path, Flik picked a seed and held it in his hand. He asked the excited young ant to describe it. The little ant rightly responded that it was a seed. In his immature mind, he could only perceive it as a small seed. He did not understand that in that seed lay great potential.

Understand that unless you identify what your real potential is, you will walk through life without enjoying the riches that your potential is meant to bring to you.

Use Your Gifts Practically

The Bible clearly makes us aware that you gain much by using your gifts. If you develop and put your talent to use it will then bring you much success (Luke 19: 12–26).

"Seest thou a man diligent in his business? He shall stand before kings; he shall not stand before mean men" (Proverbs 22: 29).

David served before Saul, the king, because he was cunning at playing the harp. Both Daniel and Joseph were excellent at interpreting dreams. Both served before kings. There is no limit to what you can accomplish if you put your talents to use. As you work with your talent, you may also one day stand before great men. You may be sought after by great people who would be desperate to benefit from your talent, and they will be willing to pay you for the services you offer. Do not dig a hole and hide your gifts. Do not miss that opportunity to work with them.

Believe in Yourself

God makes each of us unique. Our gifts are different. Even within the same environment, identical twins have different gifts. So be yourself. Look for that special quality that sets you apart from the others and enhance it. Isn't it interesting that God loves diversity? Look at the different cultures, ethnicities, skin colours, hair types, body shapes, and languages. There is an extensive variety within creation. What a wonderful God we have.

We all have different strengths and attributes. These come about because of our inherited genes, the environment we grew up in, and our various experiences.

It is not what others think of you. It is how God sees you. "Man always looketh on the outward appearance" (1 Samuel 16: 7). It means that other people's negative opinions about you may be wrong. Believe in yourself. If your confidence depends on what a man thinks about you, you will not go far in life.

Real achievers have always been single-minded, sometimes ignoring what most people think is the norm. Successful people tend to trust their hearts and instincts.

There is a reason one is born black and another white. There is a reason one living in Africa is normally dark-skinned and one created to live in temperate countries is often fair-skinned. God in his wisdom was fair and just to us all.

To give you two examples, let us examine two substances in the human body: melanin, a type of skin pigment in the skin, and brown fat, found under the skin. Black people mostly live in the tropics where we were created to dwell. The sun gives out ultraviolet light, which can cause skin cancer. Our skin appears dark because it contains the pigment melanin, which protects and prevents black people from developing skin cancer in the environment we were originally placed to dwell. You can now understand why pale-skinned people generally need sunscreen to protect their skins from excess direct UV light—because their lighter skins contain less melanin. They are at high risk of cancer.

In much the same way people created to live in cold temperate places generally tend to have fairer and lighter skin, and this gets even fairer as you travel to Western Europe. Temperate dwelling creatures tend to have more body hair because hair acts as insulation to conserve body heat. Their skin also contains more brown fat to generate more heat. Therefore, Caucasians tolerate the cold weather better than the black people who live in the tropics. Because we live in the tropics, we need less hair so we can sweat, lose heat, and maintain an ambient body temperature to prevent us dying from heat stroke.

God in his wisdom was fair and just to us all. Having dark skin is, after all, not a curse but a blessing. Begin to appreciate your elegant features because they are designed for a special reason. I feel proud to be black and would not wish to be another. I feel black and blessed and so must you wherever you come from and whatever the colour of your skin and features.

I have used this example just to illustrate how uniquely God made you and has endowed you with different gifts. Understand that you have been engineered with greatness within you. The Bible describes you as being fearfully and wonderfully made.

3

The 'Little Foxes' that Spoil Your Vine

"Take us the foxes, the little foxes that spoil the vines:
for our vines have tender grapes".

—Song of Solomon 2: 15

An interplay of several factors enables one to succeed and stay successful. I believe there is no one formula for success and no one strategy to remain at the top once you get there. It takes a combination of different factors, and when all these factors work together, at the right time and in the right season, an individual may become successful.

Some of us may not have realised our true potential, but not because we are not gifted, lack vision, or have no aim in life, but mainly because little things have become obstacles or stumbling blocks to our progress. These obstacles may be the reasons so many of us may not have fulfilled our God-given potential. Some are obvious but others are not and can become giant obstacles to our progress. For each of us it may be one, two, or a combination of any of these factors. I call them 'little foxes' because they may not be obvious but can easily wreck dreams. They are like small foxes that hide on a farm undetected yet appear at unusual times and destroy the produce.

Looking back at my own life, I have had many opportunities to have excelled to the highest level but I made slow progress. Just like the time lost when you take the wrong exit at a motorway is irrecoverable, so are missed opportunities. Sometimes you may feel like a failure and feel frustrated because you know deep within yourself that this is not the place you hoped to be in life.

You may have sought for the reason why you are not making progress and may even have pointed the finger of blame at others for your own failures. Most of us rarely point the finger of blame at ourselves. Usually someone else takes the blame for what happens to us.

If you happen to be at that crossroads now, look nowhere else but at yourself, take stock of your life, and make the needed changes.

Many of us have dreams and visions, and many of us have wishes we would like to accomplish. However, there is a huge chasm between wishing and accomplishing. It is one thing having a dream and another turning that dream into reality.

Two university graduates who studied the same courses at the same university and who both passed with distinction would graduate but have different levels of success after school. Why?

In the real world, there are determining factors. Once you leave the confines of the classroom and the comforts of your parents' home, when the supervisory roles of your teachers and parents come to an end, you suddenly find yourself on your own and at the beginning of your own journey. There are factors you will have to avoid and others you may have to adopt if your potential can truly be maximised.

The process of turning a dream into reality can be long and painful. It can be a cruel road to walk on, and many dreams have died along the way even before they began.

The following are what I call the 'little foxes' that can spoil your vine (potential, talent, and dreams). There may be other major factors, but I consider these equally important that can undermine anyone with potential. These little foxes include fear; laziness (sloth); distraction; lack of planning; lack of discipline; pride and arrogance; and a bad attitude.

As insignificant as they may sound, they make a huge difference. Having interacted with many young people, both in my clinical practice and in general life, I have been shocked to see the number of wrecked lives that could have potentially been great stories.

I have tried to explain what these factors are and offered a few tips on how we can attempt to turn our lives around.

Fear

"Fear stifles our thinking and actions. It creates indecisiveness that results in stagnation. I have known talented people who procrastinate indefinitely rather than risk failure. Lost opportunities cause erosion of confidence, and the downward spiral begins" (Pastor Charles Stanley).

What Is Fear?

The Oxford English Dictionary defines fear as "an unpleasant emotion caused by the threat of danger, pain or harm".

"Fear causes feelings of dread, apprehension, dismay, terror, fright, panic, horror, and consternation" (dictionary.com).

Fear is an emotional response when there is anticipated danger or pain or unpleasant event. It is a normal human response designed to prepare us for that perceived danger.

However, instead of fear preparing us to deal with perceived danger, it paralyses our ability to function. Fear can inhibit and limit us from fulfilling our potential. Fear is a tactic used by Satan to prevent us from stepping out in faith and claiming our God-given blessings. Fear prevents us from breaking out of our fallow grounds. It is a spirit deployed by Satan and is usually a highly effective tool that can halt our progress. Most of the things we fear hardly come to pass.

From the Anakim (descendants of the Nephilim) to Goliath, from the Egyptians to the Amalekites, from Pharaoh to Nebuchadnezzar, Satan will use anyone and anything to slow you down.

Fear creates mental and emotional distress, the anticipation of something terrible happening, and has led many to commit suicide. The thought and prospect of failure has prevented many from taking risks or taking a step of faith.

> Now after the death of Moses the servant of the Lord it came to pass, that the Lord spake unto Joshua the son of Nun, Moses' minister, saying, Moses my servant is dead; now therefore arise, go over this Jordan, thou, and all this people, unto the land which I do give to them, even to the children of Israel.
>
> Every place that the sole of your foot shall tread upon, that have I given unto you, as I said unto Moses. From the wilderness and this Lebanon even unto the great river, the river Euphrates, all the land of the Hittites, and unto the great sea toward the going down of the sun, shall be your coast.
>
> There shall not any man be able to stand before thee all the days of thy life: as I was with Moses, so I will be with thee: I will not fail thee, nor forsake thee.
>
> Be strong and of a good courage: for unto this people shalt thou divide for an inheritance the land, which I sware unto their fathers to give them. Only be thou strong and very courageous, that thou mayest observe to do according to all the law, which Moses my servant commanded thee: turn not from it to the right hand or to the left, that thou mayest prosper whithersoever thou goest.

> Have not I commanded thee? Be strong and of a good
> courage; be not afraid, neither be thou dismayed: for
> the Lord thy God is with thee whithersoever thou
> goest. (Joshua 1: 1–7, 9)

When we are faced with an unexpected situation, our first reaction is to panic. The situation occasionally forces us to make certain decisions out of fear. Fear causes us to make excuses, leads us to procrastinate, shatters our faith, and makes us lose confidence in our ability to break out and break forth. It prevents us from taking risks and creates a mental barrier (negative thoughts and imaginations) that stops us in our tracks. Fear is a spirit. This spirit prevents us from stepping out in faith to take what belongs to us on the other side of the fear barrier.

The presence of Anakim, the fear of giants, and the perceived threat of hunger, thirst, and surrounding enemies almost prevented the Israelites from possessing the land God promised—a land flowing with milk and honey. A few times they wanted to go back to Egypt (their comfort zone) without taking risks.

We become afraid of change and fail to trust God. We feed our doubts as a result of fear and so our faith grows weak. What we need to do is feed our faith and our doubts and fears will disappear.

> But the Egyptians pursued after them, all the horses
> and chariots of Pharaoh, and his horsemen, and his
> army, and overtook them encamping by the sea,
> beside Pihahiroth, before Baalzephon.
>
> And when Pharaoh drew nigh, the children of Israel
> lifted up their eyes, and, behold, the Egyptians
> marched after them; and they were sore afraid:
> and the children of Israel cried out unto the Lord.
> And they said unto Moses, because there were no
> graves in Egypt, hast thou taken us away to die in the
> wilderness? wherefore hast thou dealt thus with us,

to carry us forth out of Egypt? Is not this the word that we did tell thee in Egypt, saying, let us alone, that we may serve the Egyptians? For it had been better for us to serve the Egyptians, than that we should die in the wilderness.

And Moses said unto the people, Fear ye not, stand still, and see the salvation of the Lord, which he will shew to you today: for the Egyptians whom ye have seen today, ye shall see them again no more for ever. The Lord shall fight for you, and ye shall hold your peace. (Exodus 14: 9–14)

"And there we saw the giants, the sons of Anak, which come of the giants: and we were in our own sight as grasshoppers, and so we were in their sight" (Numbers 13: 33).

"When all Israel heard those words of the Philistine (Goliath), they were dismayed, and greatly afraid" (1 Samuel 17: 11).

Fear is usually borne out of the things we have heard or hear, seen or experienced personally. It creates anxiety and paralyses us. The people of Israel had experienced hardship at the hands of the Egyptians for years and were rightly fearful when they were being pursued as Moses led them. The ten spies were in fear of the Anakim and the sons of the giants when they saw them in the same way the words of Goliath struck fear in the armies of Israel.

Peter's experience, highlighted in Matthew 14: 26–31, buttresses this point. In this passage, Peter initially placed his faith in Christ and faced his fear of drowning in the sea. Peter took a bold step and started walking on water; he was accomplishing the impossible. Suddenly a crisis appears in the form of a boisterous wind, which caused fear, and Peter started sinking. He had allowed the storm to affect him.

I need you to understand that for as long as Peter fastened his eye on Jesus, he was accomplishing the impossible by walking on water. But as soon as he took his eye off Christ, he started sinking.

Many times, this is what happens when we allow fear to have its hold on us. It starves our faith and feeds our doubts.

Fear prevents you from taking the risks you need to take to reach the heights you need to reach. Fear can make you suddenly believe that you are worthless and a failure.

One of the real dangers about fear is that it can cause you to limit God and his ability to lead you to where He wants to take you. You need to believe that you can do all things because Jesus will strengthen you (Philippians 4: 13) and that Christ in you is greater than the power of Satan (1 John 4: 4)

Key to Overcoming Fear—the Word of God

All throughout the Bible we note that God is aware of the fear factor limiting his children from keeping their possessions. God constantly encourages us through his word not to fear but to believe. This means that he recognizes that fear can halt our progress and prevent us possessing what rightfully belongs to us. The word of God makes us courageous and bold.

God blessed Israel with everything and gave them all the promises. They were on their way to the Promised Land, but their fearful mentality could be an obstacle. They needed to be bold and needed courage to take hold of what belonged to them. They needed to be strong and courageous to face their fears and take risks, otherwise the promise would not be fulfilled.

In Joshua 1: 7, God says to Joshua: "Only be thou strong and very courageous", signalling that Joshua was likely to be overwhelmed by fear. The challenges and obstacles we are likely to face when we undertake an assignment or a risk is enough to make us fearful, so God encourages Joshua ahead of the assignment he was about to undertake.

Sometimes the conditions are conducive to doing well, but we are unable to excel because of fear. If only we can be bold enough to seize opportunities that come our way. Fear of failure can prevent a budding entrepreneur from starting a new venture or a potential pastor from starting a new church.

"And the Lord said unto Joshua, Fear not, neither be thou dismayed" (Joshua 8: 1).

The word of God is the key to overcoming fear, because fear is a spirit. God's word brings encouragement, breeds confidence, and enhances our self-esteem to the extent we are empowered to take risks.

You must cultivate the habit of making bold confessions from the word of God because the Word is God and God is Love. But we also know that 'perfect love casteth away fear'.

"In the Fear of the Lord is strong confidence" (Proverbs 14: 26). Note that the fear of the Lord is also a Spirit (Isaiah 11: 2) that helps us overcome the spirit of fear, which comes from Satan.

"I will trust, and not be afraid: for the Lord Jehovah is my strength" (Isaiah 12: 2).

"Fear not for I have redeemed thee ... when you pass through the waters, I will be with thee" (Isaiah 43: 1–2).

"For God hath not given us the spirit of fear; but of power, and of love, and of sound mind" (2 Timothy 1: 7).

This means that God gives weapons to overcome fear: the spirit of power; spirit of love; and spirit of sound mind. All three are born of God's word, and the more you meditate on his word, the more fear is cast away.

Understanding that God loves you and cares about your future takes that fear away and enables you to take risks knowing he will be with you every step of the way (Joshua 1: 6).

"There is no fear in love; but perfect love casteth away fear: because fear has torment. He that feareth is not made perfect in love" (1 John 4: 18).

Joshua and Caleb trusted in God's ability to deliver on his promises (Numbers 13: 1–33). After exploring Canaan, all twelve spies came back with their report. God had promised to bring them to a land flowing with milk and honey, and they said that indeed it was a good land flowing with milk and honey and brought along some fruits to show. But the problem was that there were obstacles to overcome to possess it—Anakim, Nephilim, giants, and powerful people as well as fortified cities—this was the source of their fear.

Caleb trusted Jehovah completely and believed they were able to possess the land (verse 30). Both Caleb and Joshua were aware of the obstacles but were also aware of God's ability to fulfil his promises (Numbers 14: 6–9). Their faith in God's word was their source of strength. The ten spies never made it to the Promised Land because of their lack of faith in God's word. Joshua and Caleb made it (Numbers 14: 38).

God appreciated Caleb's faith in him: "But my servant Caleb, because he had another spirit in him, and hath followed me fully, him will I bring into the land where into he went; and his seed shall possess it (Numbers 14: 24)

In Joshua 14: 7–8, Caleb explains that he followed God wholeheartedly and this was the key to his courage. He trusted and believed that God was able to bring him to the Promised Land.

I encourage you to trust in God's word as a way of overcoming fear. He has promised and he will not fail. Believe that God can do just what he says he will do. He will fulfil every promise to you. He will not give up on you (Numbers 23: 919; Isaiah 55: 11).

David's Exploits Were Based on His Faith in God's Word

"David said moreover, the Lord that delivered me out of the paw of the lion, and out of the paw of the bear, he will deliver me out of the hand of this Philistine" (1 Samuel 17: 37).

David acknowledged the perceived threat from the lion, the bear, and Goliath but also believed that there was a greater power that could overcome the threat he faced. He always relied on the word of God for his victories. Many times he asked for God's direction before he embarked on any major assignment. His faith in God's words filled him with courage to undertake any assignment without fear. I believe that if you can also learn to depend on the same word of God, you will have the same victories. God's word never changes.

Shadrach, Meshach, and Abednego Had Confidence that God Would Deliver Them

"If it be so, our God whom we serve is able to deliver us from the furnace, and he will deliver us out of thine hand, O King. But if not, be it known unto thee, O King, that we will not serve thy gods, nor worship the golden image which thou hast set up" (Daniel 3: 17–18).

The faith exhibited by these wonderful young men was exemplary. They were willing to stake their life against real and perceived threats whether God showed up or not. No wonder Jesus showed up and joined them in the fire. They experienced no harm (Daniel 3: 24–25). The next time you feel fearful, do not compromise your faith by making rash decisions.

I pray that the next time you are faced with a fearful situation you will trust in the word of God. May God grant you sound mind, power over adversity and show you his love to enable you overcome fear. Trust in his word that he can deliver.

Face Your Fears

"I learned that courage was not the absence of fear, but the triumph over it. The brave man is not he who does not feel afraid, but he who conquers fear" (Nelson Mandela).

I encourage you to face your fears. There is not much to lose. Even if you fail it will not be the end of life. You may learn valuable lessons and discover an inner strength and character that you never knew existed. Failure at anything is designed to make you better and push you further, if you learn the lessons it brings.

Arise and take your place. I pray that you will be empowered to do exploits. I pray for a sound mind to overcome fear and to overcome the fear of taking risks.

Prayer: Lord, give me a spirit of love, power, and soundness of mind to overcome any spirit of fear. May the Holy Spirit make me strong and of good courage. Help me overcome any real or perceived obstacles and enemies that stand in my path to progress in Jesus's name.

Laziness

A lazy, sluggard, or slothful person is one who does not like to work or use up energy to accomplish anything. Laziness is a dangerous enemy that robs many talented people and dumps them on the scrapheap of failure.

Laziness is defined by the Advanced English dictionary as "inactivity resulting from a dislike of work". It refers to a person's inability to work or use energy. A lazy person tends to be idle with very little to do. Laziness is one of the major reasons many of us are not fulfilling our potential. It is one of the commonest causes of procrastination, a reason many of us never accomplish anything, not for lack of talent or potential.

A lazy or slothful person, or sluggard, as the Bible describes him, may demonstrate one, if not all, of the characteristics listed below.

A Lazy Person Lacks Foresight or the Ability to Plan Ahead

"Go to the ant, thou sluggard; consider her ways, and be wise: which having no guide, overseer, or ruler, provideth her meat in the summer, and gathereth her food in the harvest" (Proverbs 6: 6–8).

Most lazy people are so busy idling around, doing everything and nothing. Unfortunately, when you examine the lives of most people who are poor, one thing you often see is the lack of insight or the inability to see into the future. At the time when they should work they play; when they should save, they spend; and when they should invest in their gifts, they would rather waste time. This lack of foresight makes it difficult to even take advantage of the key moments in their lives when they should invest. Usually they need a lot of pushing or pressure to get motivated (needing supervision, overseer, or a ruler).

I believe 'To provide meat in the summer and gather food in the harvest' refers to a time when one has the strength to work (and save and store or invest). There will always be a time when you earn more and a time when your sources of income will dwindle. For example, when you are young you have the strength to work harder and earn more, but as you grow older your physical abilities wane. You are unable to do the same manual work you were able to as a younger person. If your job depends on your brawn, it means that as you grow older, your ability to earn diminishes.

In difficult times it is what you have gathered that sustains you through the lean seasons. Joseph demonstrated this clearly to Pharaoh that there will always be seasons of plenty and seasons of lack (Genesis 41: 1–36). We may all go through difficult times in life, such as illness, job loss, injuries, and old age. They can affect anyone at any point and can suddenly hamper your ability to earn.

When you are younger, you have the advantage of youth and the ability to 'gather the harvest'. As you get older, gifted as you may be, the desire to gather the harvest may be there but the dynamics of old age would even hamper your efforts to 'gather'. It is why you must take advantage of youthfulness and invest in your life.

I pray that God will grant you wisdom to know when to gather and when to rest.

A Lazy Person Usually Sleeps a Lot

"How long wilt thou sleep, O sluggard? Yet a little sleep, a little slumber, a little folding of the hands to sleep" (Proverbs 6: 9–10).

Most lazy people prefer to do nothing and tend to love the leisure of sleep. They constantly moan about work, errands, studying—anything that requires effort. You are likely to find lazy people putting their feet up and relaxing than finding them putting in extra effort at making life better for themselves. They are always tired, but this is no surprise if you do not move your muscles. The body is designed for work. When muscles and joints are not used, they become rusty and stiff and will naturally cause aches and pains. If you find yourself sleeping more than you work, then know that you are slowly travelling on the road with the destination marked poverty.

You must understand that whilst rest and sleep are essential for the body and mind, excessive sleep only leads to disaster. Sleeping a lot does not necessarily lead to better health and long life. You are more likely to die from the effects of poverty than from having a little less sleep.

A Lazy Person Struggles Financially and Is Constantly in Need

"So shall thy poverty come as one that travelleth, and thy want as an armed man" (Proverbs 6: 11).

An old English proverbs states, "A young man idle, an old man needy".

Benjamin Franklin stated: "Laziness travels so slowly that poverty soon overtakes him".

In simple terms, the more you sleep, the less you can work, and in time you will be in want.

Lazy People Are Generally Full of Excuses

"The slothful man saith, there is a lion in the way; a lion is in the streets. As the door turneth upon its hinges, so doth the slothful upon his bed" (Proverbs 26: 13).

"The way of the slothful is an hedge of thorns" (Proverbs 15: 19).

"The sluggard will not plough by reason of the cold" (Proverbs 20: 4).

Lazy people are generally full of excuses why they cannot do anything or use their talents. Any perceived obstacle or threat becomes a reasonable excuse for a lazy person not to do something that requires effort. Every perceived difficult task or challenge is like a lion (an insurmountable situation or problem).

The lazy person will blame everything and everyone—the 'system', their background, the boss, his wife, her husband, and even the in-laws—as the main reason they are not progressing in life. They would use any little hindrance as an excuse not to work or help themselves. You are more likely to hear lazy people blame others than look at themselves. Every job is hard, every assignment is not ideal, and every task given to them is like a chore.

As soon as they sense a little obstacle, they are likely to exaggerate the situation (a lion) and find reasons why it cannot be done. They are likely to sound pessimistic about a new idea, a new move or assignment than take risks. Quite simply because they must put in effort to do something or make sacrifices, they are more likely to discourage others from that assignment or find reasons why it cannot be done.

Lazy people may end up doing jobs they may not want to do

"The hand of the diligent shall bear rule but the slothful shall be under tribute" (Proverbs 12: 24).

"The sluggard will not plough by reason of the cold; therefore shall he beg in harvest, and have nothing" (Proverbs 20: 4).

This may not necessarily happen directly in the advanced world, but in most third-world countries, it is not unusual to find poor people having to make regular payments to landowners, property owners, or loan sharks. If you are lazy, you are more likely to find yourself doing menial jobs to survive or do things you may not want to do. A lazy Christian, out of need, may have to compromise his or her faith, integrity, and personal freedom. Poverty makes you vulnerable and places you at the mercy of wicked and unreasonable people. Poverty may force people to do things they may not want to do just to survive. When you are in need, you will do anything to survive if there are no options. If you are reading this book, I need you to understand that if you do not utilize your talents or do something worthwhile with your life, you will end up one day living on the scrapheap of poverty.

Lazy People Do Not Value What They Have and Fail to Develop Their Potential

"I went by the field of the slothful, and by the vineyard of the man void of understanding; and, lo, it was all grown over with thorns, and nettles had covered the face thereof, and the stone wall thereof was broken down" (Proverbs 24: 30–34).

It can be seen from this scripture that every lazy person also has a gift or talent to work on. Most lazy people have had opportunities to do well. The lazy person also has a field or vineyard but fails to develop that vineyard. That vineyard may be your talent, resources, or even an inheritance that you have been given.

They cannot perceive that they have a talent just like everyone else. Lazy people tend to lack the understanding that the field or vineyard (potential) must be developed. They will allow it (talent, inheritance, opportunities) to lie fallow, undeveloped or untapped. Because of sheer laziness, what could have been a blessing is devalued and allowed to go to waste. If you leave an inheritance or treasure in the care of a lazy person, it will in no time be wasted.

The scripture highlights the effects of laziness on our gifts, potentials, or valuable things. Too much sleep and relaxation and a lack of understanding of your God-given inheritance will rob you of a future blessing. Laziness can rob a minister with potential of his or her greatness simply because he or she cannot spend time to read the Bible or pray or improve his or her ministry. Laziness can prevent your promotion at work.

You can see examples of people who were given an inheritance, a position, a church, a fellowship, an organization, or something to manage. Like the servant who hid the talent given to him, most lazy people, given something precious to manage, will waste it. Then they will blame their boss, manager, spouse, the organization, and everyone but themselves.

I believe that when things do not work in your life, the first person to look at is yourself. Bad bosses blame those around them, never themselves. A bad worker always blames his or her tools.

If you have money, don't give it to a lazy or slothful person to manage because that person will waste it.

"By much slothfulness the building decayeth; and through idleness of the hands the house droppeth through" (Ecclesiastes 10: 18).

I pray that you will not allow laziness to rob you of your future. Spend your time wisely to invest in your potential, and not sleep a lot. Do not allow too much idleness and sleep to rob you of a great future. Do something with your life or you will one day end up in poverty. Do not allow 'nettles' and 'thorns' to destroy your vineyard or field.

Rise up and take your rightful place, and may the Holy Spirit give you the grace to break out and break forth.

It is my prayer that you will be stirred up to wake up from your slumber, from always crossing your arms, and from always making excuses. Use your God-given gifts. I rebuke any spirit of laziness that has had any negative effect on your life in Jesus's name.

Overcoming Laziness—the Keys to Hard Work and Sacrifice

Two important factors are required to move an average non-achieving person from ordinary to extraordinary.

To become extraordinary and victorious, you need that extra factor (X-factor) to propel you. If you want to move higher in life or upwards in whatever you do, you need to change some things about yourself. You cannot remain at the same level, doing the same things day in and day out and expect a better result. This is because if you do the same things every day, you will get the same results every day. What you put in is what you get out. The Bible makes this fact clear: "Be not deceived, God is not mocked: whatsoever a man soweth that shall he also reap" (Galatians 6: 7). Simply put, if you sow the wind, you reap the wind.

What Does the Bible Say about Hard Work?

In John 12: 24, Jesus said, "Verily, verily, I say unto you, except a corn of wheat falls into the ground and die, it abideth alone".

"But by the Grace of God I am what I am: and his Grace which was bestowed on me was not in vain; but I laboured more abundantly than they all: yet not I, but the grace of God which was with me" (1 Corinthians 15: 10 KJV).

I want us to examine this scripture because the apostle Paul highlights a few important things. He states that God makes grace available to us all. Unmerited favour has been made available for everyone. Grace comes in so many forms—time, strength, opportunities, skill, health, as a job, or having key people around you. All this is made available to you because God desires that we do well. Because of God's new mercies each day, even when we waste them, he still gives us chances. He continually shows favour. But a time comes when the grace may not be available anymore because with each passing day we grow older, and despite having zeal, we would not accomplish much. I believe that even before you start on your journey, God stations helpers along the way so that for every step you take in faith, there is help along the way.

Paul also talks about sheer hard work as a key to his exploits (1 Corinthians 15: 10). He tries not to sound proud because sometimes when you point out this fact, you may sound as if you are boasting about the concept of hard work.

However, the Bible makes it clear that hard work is a requirement. God is wise and designed that working is vital for the function of the body otherwise disease sets in.

So even though God will provide, most of the work must be done by yourself. It is clear in the Bible that if you do not work hard, poverty shall overcome you like an armed bandit and in a while you will be in need. You cannot blame anyone but yourself if you die, make it to heaven, and realize that you were destined for greatness but failed because you did not put in the hard work required.

"For a dream cometh through the multitude of business (the AMP version says "through much effort")" (Ecclesiastes 5: 3).

Between the early and latter rain there is a period of unfruitfulness, a period when the hard work has to be done. When the seed sprouts from the ground it is very tender and competes with weeds and other similar seedlings for water, space, nutrients, and sunshine. It struggles to establish itself amongst other seedlings. How much fruit it yields for the farmer, the one who invested in the farm, depends on how much effort the farmer puts in to ensure that this seedling has access to everything it needs. Because both the former and latter rain may fall, but if the soil has not been prepared, the seedling may not benefit from the rains. I am talking about the hard work you need to put in yourself to make that dream happen.

"Wealth gotten by vanity shall be diminished: but he that gathereth by labour shall increase" (Proverbs 13: 11). Hard work and sacrifice go hand in hand. As you work hard you make sacrifices, but if you are not willing to make sacrifices, you will not work hard.

At some point, an opportunity for success will come. However, to make that opportunity count, there should have been preparation. Opportunity plus preparation equals success. Ability and hard work with sacrifice leads to success. Some may get so far with ability alone, and still others may get far with sheer hard work and a good attitude though they possess average ability. Occasionally, average people put 100 per cent into what they are doing, and they believe in it, so they fulfil their potential.

If a person with talent or ability combines his or her ability with hard work and a good attitude, the sky is the limit. A combination of these factors will ensure extraordinary, long-lasting success.

Distraction (Lack of Focus)

The Advanced Dictionary defines distraction as "drawing someone's attention away from something". The Oxford English Dictionary defines distraction as "a thing that prevents someone from concentrating on something else".

Distraction affects our potential in a significant way because it causes divided attention. It prevents us from focusing on projects and completing assignments. Distraction affects a person's decisiveness.

Some people never make up their minds about what they want to do in life. They are never able to focus on developing their potential. Rather than focusing on one project at a time, they try to develop many things at once. They keep moving from one project to another, one course after another, from one business to another and never deciding on anything.

"It's important to focus on what we do best and master one craft at a time. A clear and focused mind will last a lifetime. Getting your mind in shape is nothing less than the key to sustainable success in the world" (Russell Simmons).

When you are easily distracted, and you lack focus, you are described as being double-minded. "A double minded man is unstable in all his ways" (James 1: 8).

So many things that can distract us, and almost everything we are exposed to appears appealing. Have you ever attended an open day at a university or secondary school? Every school presents itself as the best. But if you do a little research, you will always find that not everything you were told by the school was the truth. We are saturated with a lot of information from the Internet, news media, books, and many other sources. Without the ability to be selective, you can be led astray.

Many people are distracted by television, advertisements, and entertainment and spend so much time browsing the Internet or spending time on Facebook, Twitter, Snapchat, Instagram, and Netflix, to name a few. They spend less time reading, learning, and developing their potential. They would rather be on social media. We are told to 'chillax' rather than invest our time wisely. We are bombarded with exciting box set TV programs rather than materials to enhance learning. We need to stay focused.

Some of us are distracted by our failures, but we must learn to focus on our victories or successes. Your mistakes can be a distraction and prevent you from progressing. Remember that everyone has made mistakes and likely experienced some sort of setback.

Luke 10: 39–42 tells the story of Mary and Martha and when Jesus visited. Martha was so cumbered (distracted) about many things. Mary chose to listen to the Word, which Jesus described as being needful. What Martha was doing was also very needful; after all, she was preparing to host Jesus and anxiety consumed her. At that moment, Mary chose to listen to the Master speak and think about refreshments afterwards.

Being easily distracted is also a sign of immaturity. Children are easily distracted and often lack the ability to focus. When a child wants a toy, he or she will throw tantrums to get it, but after a few hours will lose interest in playing with it. Children have short attention spans and cannot stay at one task for a long time.

Overcoming Distraction—Keys to Sharpen Focus and Concentration

The key to sharpening focus and concentration enables us to overcome distractions. Being able to focus on the task at hand or the vision at present will allow you to accomplish one thing at a time. Staying faithful and true to your vision and giving it your best efforts will help you see that vision through to its end.

"If therefore thine eye be single, thy whole body shall be full of light.... No man can serve two masters: for either he will hate the one and love the other; or else he will hold to the one and despise the other" (Matthew 6: 22, 24). The emphasis here is on focusing on one thing at a time. You must have a 'single eye' to see a vision through.

A focused mind is devoid of distractions. A mind that is focused stays faithful to a vision until it reaches the desired outcome. A focused mind allows you to overcome many obstacles that appear insurmountable.

The decision to be committed to something or be focused on just one mission, objective, or endeavour will not come easily. Staying focused is a personal decision and a commitment you must make. It will not come automatically. It requires a lot of willpower to lead a focused life without being distracted.

Many of us remember the story of Ruth and Orpah in the Bible (book of Ruth). Both young ladies were faced with a dilemma: if they opted to stay with Naomi, their mother -in-law, they were likely to remain single and widowed for the rest of their lives. Or they could remarry and move on.

Naomi gave both women an option to make a decision that would impact their lives. The choices they made were starkly different and profound. Orpah decided to remain in Moab rather than accompany Naomi back to her country. She had thoughts about not remaining single for the rest of her life and wanted to get married again and have children. She wanted a 'normal' life again. After all, she was still young, and you cannot criticise or condemn her for wanting to get married again and have children.

Ruth made her decision based on her commitment to Naomi. Rather than seek a new adventure, a new dream, or a new venture, she made up her mind to stay with Naomi despite the obvious consequence that she might remain a widow for the rest of her life. She sacrificed her freedom, liberty, dreams, and vision to serve Naomi, whose needs she placed above her own. Having weighed all the options, and possibly influenced by her love, compassion, and devotion to Naomi, she decided to remain faithful and committed to Naomi and was blessed.

What this story teaches is that remaining faithful to something, just that one thing, will eventually bring rewards if we do not lose faith. This is how life's rewards can be reaped if many of us can abide for years doing the same things over and over.

Any time you apply for a job, two of the important pieces of information you are usually asked to provide as part of the application and résumé process: previous addresses over the past five years and previous employment history. Do you know why? I believe those two questions give an indication of how committed and stable a person is.

For example, if a person has worked for the same firm and lived at the same address for the past five years, chances are he or she is committed and stable. That sort of person, if employed, is likely to remain in the firm for a long while and is also the type of person you can train and invest in. No company would like to employ a person who changes jobs and addresses every six to twelve months. That sort of person is unstable, cannot make up his or her mind, and can be easily distracted by a better situation elsewhere. This person is likely to move on any time. You cannot invest in such a person.

"The righteous shall flourish like the palm tree: he shall grow like a cedar in Lebanon. Those that be planted in the house of the Lord shall flourish in the courts of our God. They shall still bring forth fruit in old age; they shall be fat and flourishing" (Psalm 92: 12–14).

There are two key lessons in this scripture. You must have the characteristics of stability and faithfulness to do well, and long-term stability leads to long-term success. Stability and faithfulness in any endeavour result in fruitfulness. Being faithful, loyal, and consistent to a specific vision results in success. Be decisive and not easily distracted. Make up your mind about what you want to become in life, and by God's grace you will fulfil his purpose for your life.

The reality is that any business you do can succeed if you stay focused. Whether you want to start a church, sell water or bread, roast chicken, or sell dog chains, you can succeed at anything if you remain faithful to the vision. Do not let anything or anyone distract you. Just stay focused, believe in your dream, and watch it succeed. Stay at it until you see the desired results.

God has promised in his Word (Bible) that you will do well. You are already destined for greatness and programmed to achieve great things.

"For I know the plans and thoughts that I have for you, says the Lord, plans for peace and well-being and not for disaster, to give you a future and a hope" (Jeremiah 29: 11 AMP).

"Though thy beginning was small (or insignificant), yet thy latter end shall greatly increase" (Job 8: 7 KJV).

These are promises from his word that you must believe. To be able to break out and break forth, you need total focus and concentration on your assignments or goals. Avoid distractions. Remain faithful to that dream.

It is my prayer that the Holy Spirit will work on your mind and take away any spirit of distraction. May your mind be focused on God and things that are important in your life in Jesus's name. Amen.

Lack of Planning

The Advanced English dictionary defines planning as "an act of formulating a program for a definite course of action. It is the process of thinking about what you will do in the event of something happening". This means that once you have a vision, what follows next is planning to accomplish that vision.

Planning is important and requires time and commitment of resources. Before you embark on any important assignment, you must sit down and analyse what you want to do and formulate a plan on how to accomplish it. It also allows you also put measures in place in case something goes wrong, because every journey is beset by obstacles. The best made plans do not always happen as we want them to.

In the business world, a crucial aspect of planning involves what is called doing a SWOT (strengths, weaknesses, opportunities, and threats) analysis before beginning a new project. This analysis can show signs that the business will succeed or fail.

Doing a SWOT at a personal level allows you to assess your strengths (for example, resources you possess to accomplish the project), weaknesses (such as any bad habits that may be a disadvantage), and opportunities or threats that your dream faces.

Unfortunately, many of us take off without any form of planning and then, midway through the project, everything comes to a standstill.

Many of us do not fulfil our potential or reach the heights we want because we do not really think about what we are doing. Is it a business you are starting, a course you are undertaking, a church you are beginning, or a marriage you are contemplating?

Planning is not an excuse to procrastinate fulfilling your vision. Many dreams have been possibly wrecked because we just rushed into things without doing any analysis.

The Key to Planning: Do Not Leave Your Future to Chance

A failure to prepare means preparing to fail in life. Planning is an excellent key. You must be able to take stock of your life at every stage and analyse your progress every step of the way to see how far you have come. Planning carefully does not mean procrastinating, and it certainly does not mean go slowly. It helps to know what you are doing every step of your journey. It helps you execute the vision you have mapped in front of you.

What the Bible Says about Planning

"For which of you, intending to build a tower, sitteth not down first, and counteth the cost, whether he have sufficient to finish it? Lest haply, after he hath laid the foundation, and is not able to finish it, all that behold it begin to mock him, saying, this man began to build, and was not able to finish" (Luke 14: 28–30).

Here, Jesus was teaching us not to suddenly rush into things but to carefully consider any venture we like to undertake and plan before embarking on that vision. This is wisdom, and it also takes wisdom to know what it will cost to get where you want to go and prepare adequately for the trip.

Many of us took courses in university without thinking through the decision we were making. You never discussed them with anyone, never considered how employable you would be in the future doing that coursework, or never wondered whether you could progress in life pursuing a career in that field.

Stay true to your own vision and you may be proved right. Before you embark on any venture, do some planning. Speak to people who have done what you want to do, get their views and opinions, and then decide. It will ensure that you make fewer mistakes on your way to fulfilling your potential.

"Any enterprise is built by wise planning, it becomes strong through the use of common sense, and profits wonderfully by keeping abreast of the facts" (Proverbs 24: 3–4 New Living Translation).

I pray that you will be filled with wisdom and that any spirit of disorganization and confusion be taken away from your mind, in Jesus's name. I pray that the Holy Spirit will give you the gift of planning as you strive to fulfil your potential. Amen.

Lack of Discipline, Diligence, and Commitment

Discipline

The Oxford English Dictionary define discipline as "Training oneself to do something in a controlled and habitual way". The definition mentions two key words: control and habit. To be disciplined, you need to abide by a system of rules by which you conduct yourself or live your life in a controlled and habitual way. Without any form of discipline, it is likely that you may not be able attain your goals and achieve high levels of success.

An average footballer may continue to be average, and his career will not last long, if he does not stay away from drugs, junk food, alcohol, and smoking. Without discipline and studying, a good student will fail his or her exams. A person who is not disciplined with money may end up poor. Without discipline in many areas of their lives, successful businesspeople, sportspeople, ministers, or politicians will likely find their careers unsuccessful.

Discipline enables an individual to maintain a certain level of self-control.

Without this rigid code of conduct or behaviour, you may not be able to accomplish what you set out to do. You need to train yourself mentally and physically to endure pain and mental stress. This is because you will need to overcome some tough challenges as you rise.

Disciplining oneself is not pleasant, but it can be rewarding. The hallmark of discipline is the ability to sacrifice life's little pleasures if you want to achieve anything. For example, too much sleep, leisure, pleasure, wastefulness, or laziness can wreck any potential.

Without discipline, a gifted person can easily lead a reckless life full of reckless habits, which eventually will wreck his or her potential. Without discipline, a good marriage can be destroyed by a careless one-night stand, a pastor's ministry can be derailed by a careless moment of passionate embrace (the pleasure that thrills is the pleasure that kills), and a gifted athlete can suddenly wreck his or her career because of a lack of discipline.

"Can a man hold fire against his chest without burning his clothes? Can a man walk on hot coals without scorching his feet?" (Proverbs 6: 27–28 NET).

If you are a student, you must study to pass your exams. If you decide to spend your time having fun, you will likely fail.

"For sound advice is a beacon, good teaching is a light, moral discipline is a life path" (Proverbs 6: 23 The Message).

"Foolishness is bound up in the heart of a child; The rod of discipline [correction administered with godly wisdom and lovingkindness] will remove it far from him (Proverbs 22: 15 AMP).

"A refusal to correct is a refusal to love; love your children by disciplining them" (Proverbs 13: 24 The Message).

"Discipline your children while you still have a chance; indulging them destroys them" (Proverbs 19: 18 The Message).

"Do not withhold discipline from a child; if you strike him with a rod, he would not die. If you strike him with a rod, you will save his soul from Sheol" (Proverbs 23: 13–14 ESV).

The Bible describes discipline as a rod that drives away foolishness. This means discipline is a kind of antidote that will drive away the foolish things that can destroy your future. Disciplining yourself is almost like striking yourself with a rod.

There is always the natural tendency to live a life of relaxation, especially in today's world where we are encouraged to 'chillax'. Modern electronic gadgets and forms of entertainment make it so easy to slip into a routine of relaxation, which can be disastrous. Advancements in science and technology have created a lazy, undisciplined generation who get stressed too easily. They find it stressful to study, wake up to learn, sit for prolonged periods of time to research, and tire easily when they are stretched a little physically. They are a generation that loves a little sleep and a little slumber and a little fun. If you want to fulfil your God-given potential, great discipline is required. It will be painful but worthwhile in the end.

As a teenager, I failed some of my GCE O level subjects on the first attempt because I lapsed into a life of pleasure at a crucial time when I should have been studying. I was in boarding school all through my secondary education. From years 7 to 9 I was quite studious and disciplined, helped by the fact that I came from a working-class background and did not have the financial resources like other students to go out into the town to have fun.

However, during the summer holidays at the end of year 9, I had the opportunity to visit the United Kingdom for the first time. When I went back to school in Ghana, my behaviour changed. I lost my self-discipline, which had always been a cornerstone for my small academic achievements during my early years. I started absconding from the boarding school at night and occasionally during the day to watch movies and have fun. I continued this bad behaviour even in year 11 when I was supposed to revise for my GCSE. Unsurprisingly, my standards dropped, and I failed in some subjects, which delayed my entry to sixth form.

Life was very tough in the intervening years without any direction, GCSE, or an apprenticeship. By the grace of God I was fortunate enough to have counsel at the right time from different sources. I was able to reflect on where I had gone wrong and had a second chance at resitting my GCSE. This time I did not mess around and have continued in the same discipline for the rest of my life.

However, not everyone gets a second chance at making a U-turn. Not everyone is fortunate enough to recover when they make a wrong turn. You may not be as fortunate as I was in having good people around to speak to your life and help get you back on track. That lack of discipline took three crucial years and possibly changed the course of my life. All great people have stated time and time again that discipline is one of the keys to great accomplishments.

Joseph (Genesis 39: 6–12) is a good example of a person with discipline. I believe that other than his fear of God, he was aware that a great destiny lay ahead of him. He was so disciplined and committed to his job that not even the temptation of sex could derail his dream. Potiphar's wife tried to lure him to have 'guilty pleasures' but failed despite the daily pressure she put on Joseph.

No one was watching on that day. The house was empty, and of course there were no cameras to record any orgies—no selfies, and no evidence. He could have bowed to the pressure and along with it the 'perks' of being the 'sugar boy' of the boss's wife.

Some mere mortals like us have succumbed to the temptation. Joseph was probably fully aware of the huge price to pay for any error of judgement: embarrassment, prison, or even death. He knew this abominable thing would have ended his dream, destroyed his potential, and ended his life. He had to keep his body under real discipline not to succumb to the woman's sexual advances.

Joseph did not bow to pressure. He kept his godly discipline when no one was watching. And this is the key. The ability to maintain your discipline when no one is around to watch, supervise, encourage, or pat you on the back. It was no mean task to achieve for this young man, but his faithfulness to his master, his personal godly discipline, and his fear of God took him to the very top.

Champions are truly made when no one is watching. Everyone is equipped with some resilience, and only you can make that decision to stay disciplined. No one can do that for you.

Daniel and others did not obey the command to eat food sacrificed for idols. That was godly discipline. Joseph's refusing to sleep with Potiphar's wife was godly discipline.

American businessman and author Harvey Mackay stated, "It doesn't matter whether you are pursuing success in business, sports, the arts, or life in general: the bridge between wishing and accomplishing is discipline."

Discipline will enable you to train when others are asleep, invest time and effort into that business or project when others are relaxing, and study past midnight when others are asleep. Discipline will ensure that you use your time wisely rather than spending hours on social media and watching useless movies, which would not in any way enhance your productivity. Personal discipline will enable you to manage your time well.

Diligence

Diligence refers to the ability to focus on a task and having the determination to see it accomplished.

The Oxford English Dictionary also defines diligence as "careful and persistent work or effort".

I realize that if you do not make a conscious effort to see something through, chances are you will give up along the way. Diligence helps you to see the task to the very end. It helps prevent distraction, enhances your focus, and ensures that your progress is not derailed. If the effort you put into a task, business, studies, or venture is persistent, it may eventually pay off. Your diligence will likely ensure that you excel.

"Seest thou a man diligent at his business? He shall stand before kings; he shall not stand before mean men" (Proverbs 22: 29).

"Behold, I have seen a son of Jesse the Bethlehemite, that is cunning in playing" (1 Samuel 16: 16).

"And Saul sent to Jesse, saying, Let David, I pray thee, stand before me; for he hath found favour in my sight" (1 Samuel 16: 22).

The scriptures confirm that people who pay attention to what they are doing and persists at it will go to the very top of their profession. At that level, it is 'kings' who seek to benefit from your services and your talents.

I believe David never gave up practicing his harp as he tended the sheep. You do not become skilled or cunning at an activity overnight. It takes a lot of practice. The more you rehearse something, the more skilful you become. Becoming 'cunning' at anything takes a lot of sacrifice and time, which is why patience is required. There was possibly no one around to encourage him, but as he watched the sheep feed, he kept practicing. He knew how to encourage himself—it's called self-motivation. You don't always have someone encouraging you all the way to the top. In fact, most times the road to the top can be lonely. You may need to plug away alone, like a seed buried in the dark soil, waiting for the right time to burst out. When it does burst out, it grows slowly until one day it blossoms.

As you teach that small group, or preach to that small church, or do Holy Ghost baptism for those few church members, week after week, remember that you are rehearsing for a greater future. Just do not give up.

I pray that during those difficult moments, when you feel like giving up, may God be your source of strength. Do not give up; persevere, and even if you don't succeed initially, you will one day find yourself at your summit. It is at that point that you may reap the rewards of your hard work. That is when fame knocks at your door and everyone seeks to be part of your success.

Diligence breeds consistency, which eventually results in success. Therefore, whatever you are doing, try to be diligent. Any great accomplishment is done at great cost. Whenever you see a great person who has accomplished great things, you must understand that he or she has done so at great price.

It takes great mental strength not to give up on a vision, venture, or project when faced with obstacles. However, you can make strides with a persevering determination. A lack of diligence could result in wasted opportunities.

Commitment

Commitment means being dedicated to a cause or activity. Commitment will push your dream further than mere desire.

Stay at something until it bears fruit. Everything works if you persist at it. Have the patience to allow it to get better. Do not be in a hurry to succeed. Be faithful to the dream until it is accomplished and persevere until you see what you want to see. Travail until the birthed vision bears fruit or produces the desired results. Learn to stay the course because medals are only given to those who finish a race, not those who give up along the way. Be fully dedicated and committed to your vision.

Like a Good Recipe

When you are preparing a good stew (depending on how you were taught), the ingredients are added one after the other in a certain order. As the ingredients are put in, it is initially tasteless. However, by the time the stew is finished, a nice, tasty meal is produced. The final taste is because of the effect of the heat and the interaction of the different flavours and juices from the individual ingredients.

In the same way, it appears almost impossible to succeed or fulfil any great potential without discipline, commitment, diligence, hard work, and sacrifice. These five qualities appear to go hand in hand. There are no shortcuts. To make it to the top, you need all five qualities.

Gifted as you may be, if you lack these qualities, then your 'vineyard' will be overgrown with thorns. This means that no matter what talent you have or inheritance is given to you, it will be wasted in the absence of those factors. The Bible does not lie.

Do you remember the story of the grasshopper and the ant? When the grasshopper was having fun, the ant was tempted to ask itself whether it was missing out on fun. But as the seasons changed, the wisdom and benefit of the ant's discipline made a difference. Do not waste your potential and throw away your future.

Remember this, by Henry Wadsworth Longfellow: "The heights that great men reached and kept were not attained by sudden flight, but they, while their companions slept, kept toiling upward in the night".

It is my fervent prayer that you stay true to your vision, maintain your discipline, and be dedicated to the dream and you will be surprised by the great accomplishments God will bring your way.

Pride

"When pride cometh, then cometh shame: but with the lowly is wisdom" (Proverbs 11: 2).

"Pride goeth before destruction, and a haughty spirit before a fall" (Proverbs 16: 18).

Promotion, riches, fame, power, and praise have a way of making us proud. Our status in society, the circles we move in, and even the locality in which we live can make us proud. Some take pride in their beauty, others in their intelligence. All of us have things we feel proud about.

But I am not talking about the pride that comes with success, because most people naturally become proud with some level of achievement.

I am referring to the foolish pride and arrogance that become obstacles to progress, the kind of pride and arrogance that prevent a young person or apprentice from being trained or guided. I am talking about the know-it-all attitude and arrogance that have hindered the development and promotion of many a gifted person.

Pride and arrogance are subtle, sometimes not easily detected. Pride causes us to be rebellious, to reject advice and correction, and to prevent us from being apologetic. Once you allow pride into your life, you are on a path to destruction. In a matter of years, your life will be wrecked.

The Sad Story of Humpty Dumpty

"Humpty Dumpty sat on a wall; Humpty Dumpty had a great fall. All the King's horses and all the king's men couldn't put Humpty together again".

Most of us know this nursery rhyme. Humpty (in my humble opinion) could also represent a proud person who sits on this 'high wall' above everyone. They like to take the moral high ground; they know it all and can do no wrong—until disaster strikes. And when they fall (the higher the wall, the greater the fall) the damage is often irreparable. Sometimes the damage is so irreparable that no amount of help (all the king's horses and men) can put them together. That is why you must remain humble and continue learning (Jeremiah 50: 31–32).

The Apprentice Carpenter

Many years ago, I heard the story of two young apprentices who were learning their trade under a master craftsman.

They were learning their trade in the upholstery business. They had different attitudes towards their master. One had an 'I know it all' attitude, and any time the master taught them, he did not pay attention. I will call him Mr Proud. His body language suggested he did not want to be there. He also did not ask any questions during the sessions, an indication that he did not think there was anything new that could be added to his knowledge. His pride was such that he felt that the old craftsman could not teach him anymore than he already knew. However, the other apprentice (Mr Humble) had an excellent spirit, a teachable spirit, always eager to listen, and eager to learn new things, eager to question even when he knew the answer and more importantly demonstrated openly that he was willing to be taught and serve as an apprentice. Not surprising, Mr Proud was always in a hurry to leave the apprenticeship and will always leave at exactly 5pm each day as soon as the day ends. The apprentice with the spirit of servitude would however stay behind after 5pm, always asking the master if there was anything extra, he could do.

As the years passed, the master appreciated the attitude and humility of this humble apprentice and his desire to serve, learn, and be taught.

In the final two years of their apprenticeship, he started teaching Mr Humble the secrets of the trade, but always after 5pm when Mr Proud had left. During the day he would teach them the basic knowledge required in the upholstery business, but after 5pm he would spend more time with Mr Humble, pouring out years of experience, expertise, secrets, contacts, to-dos, what not to do, and mistakes to avoid in the trade. Interestingly, he swore this humble apprentice to secrecy and to not ever impart this knowledge to the proud apprentice.

After four years of training, it was time for both apprentices to graduate. Before they both took leave, the master asked both the same question: What are your plans? Unsurprisingly, Mr Proud was the first to speak. He had his own plans. He was going to find a loan and start his own business. However, Mr Humble responded that he did not really know what his next steps were and asked the master that if it was not too much to ask, could he stay on for a little while because he felt he was not yet the finished article. (Proverbs 20: 5)

He wanted to be like his master before leaving.

At that point, the master looked at both, and with his gaze fixed on Mr Humble, he told them he was now old and after all these years had decided to retire from the trade. He was wealthy but had neither child nor next of kin to inherit the business. Having worked and trained so many apprentices through the years, he had always sought somebody he could leave his inheritance to. He pointed to Mr Humble and told him that he felt he was the best person to oversee his business, and if it were not too much to ask, would he want to be the son he never had?

I leave what happened next to your own imagination.

Pride acts like a barrier that prevents us from learning or being taught. It blocks advice from getting to us because our judgement is always clouded by a bloated ego and overestimation of who we really are. You can sometimes observe a proud person hurting or self-destructing, yet he or she cannot accept help. They need a helping hand, but none is stretched towards them because they find it so difficult to be humble. You are likely to be left on your own to self-destruct because no one knows what your reaction will be when corrected or rebuked.

If you are proud, you are also unlikely to be receptive to advice from those deemed 'inferior' to you. You are likely to lose out on key information, coming from those above and around you, that would have been a blessing to you.

"The patient in spirit is better than the proud in spirit" (Ecclesiastes 7: 8–9).

You need to understand you can learn from virtually anybody and that you do not know it all. Remember also that even if you are from a privileged background, you will always need people. You will always need the input of people great and small. Just as your rich and famous connections can push you ahead, less wealthy, or even poor people can make you better. There is always a reason God brings all manner of people around us, and failure to acknowledge their input may one day lead to disaster.

Keys to Humility and Servanthood are Keys to Overcoming Pride and Arrogance

"A man's pride shall bring him low: but honour shall uphold the humble in spirit" (Proverbs 29: 23).

Much has been said about humility and developing the attitude of a 'servant'. Servanthood and humility go hand in hand with another quality called submissiveness. We tend to use the term, especially in marriage, because it involves a union of two partners in a relationship that requires one to lead and the other to follow. A rich parent may decide to leave an inheritance to a servant rather than his or her own child because of disrespect, dishonour, and gross insolence from that child, and an insolent, arrogant employee will never be promoted (and would likely be terminated if that employee didn't adjust his or her attitude). Nobody wants a rebellious person around.

Learning to serve and be submissive is an art that can be learnt even if you are not blessed with the spirit of humility. And learn you must, otherwise you will only get to a certain point in life and get stuck.

Jesus likened the attitude of a servant to that of a child (Mark 9: 31–36). Children are gullible and believe almost anything, until they work out that the Christmas presents under the tree are placed there by mum and dad and not Santa Claus.

The servant's spirit is one of dependence on his or her master. A servant does not pretend to know more than the master even though in some cases the servant may have more insight and experience at dealing with an issue. Jesus taught that if you want to lead, you must first learn to serve.

In John 13: 4–8, Jesus taught Peter the principle of serving your way to the top. If you don't, you will be a fake and inexperienced successful person prone to mistakes and rash decisions. When you have not risen through the ranks and earned the right to lead, your legitimacy will be questioned. It is why Jacob had to serve Laban; Joseph had to serve the midianites and portiphar and as a steward in prison; Moses had to serve Jethro, and David had to work his way through the ranks. There is no other way. Even Jesus served his disciples. Either you humbly serve your way up or you will be forced to do so through adversity. You must serve your way to the top. You must start small and finish big. The way to the top starts from the bottom.

Humility is a great spiritual quality. It is a divine strength, not a weakness; a sign of maturity, not foolishness; and one of the essential requirements for longer lasting success. You should never feel ashamed to serve under anybody. It is always an opportunity to learn and become better because you can learn many things from everybody around you.

Humility means so much to God that it is mentioned often in the Bible and many stories refer to it. The Bible uses words such as lifting up, exalting, grace, greatest, and honour with being humble. In short, humility will inevitably lead to promotion in life.

The Humility of Esther and the Demotion of Vashti

Queen Vashti forgot that she owed her promotion, position, and fame to her husband, King Ahasuerus. She made the mistake of thinking that she was possibly equal in rank. One moment of careless pride and she was replaced. She lost her place, her position, and the prestige she enjoyed. Her place was given to a 'better' woman (Esther 1: 19).

How could Esther possibly be better than Vashti? After all, she was an uneducated orphan who was not any closer to royalty than I am to Buckingham palace but was selected to replace Queen Vashti. How is it that many beautiful and well-educated wives or even husbands have been replaced by alternatives who were less endowed with beauty, intelligence, or education?

But Esther was a humble young lady, very respectful and obedient to her uncle Mordecai's counsel. Even when the time came for her to go to the king, she relied on the counsel and direction of Hegai, the king's chamberlain (Esther 2: 15–17). Esther was humble enough to listen to, learn from, and obey those more experienced than her. Her beauty (2: 7) did not make her proud. She always obeyed Mordecai (2: 20). Her humility brought her honour, and her submissiveness led to promotion. She qualified to replace Vashti because of her humility (Proverbs 29: 23; James 4: 10).

The Submissiveness of Ruth

Like Esther, Ruth was humble and submissive. Like Esther, she also hearkened to counsel given by Naomi, who was more experienced. Ruth believed in Naomi and was convinced that her destiny was tied with Naomi. She was so committed that nothing would sway her decision (Ruth 1: 18). That sort of commitment is not common and was eventually rewarded. Boaz was attracted to her humility, attitude, and servitude (2: 11–12).

Ruth followed every bit of advice her mother-in-law gave her and every instruction Boaz gave her on the field. No wonder Boaz was so eager to marry her, whether she was a widow or not. Remember, she was a Moabitess, the tribe cursed by God, yet found herself in the genealogy of Jesus by becoming the grandmother of King David. Having honoured the spiritual laws of humility, submissiveness, and obedience, God had no choice but to bless her. You will also be blessed and promoted if you follow the same time-tested spiritual principles.

The Repentant Attitude of Naaman

Sadly, many people tend to associate humility with those who are poor or needy, which is why it is often seen as a weakness and not a strength. However, there are also notable people in the Bible who were great yet humble. Moses is described as such. David's humility made it possible for him to receive counsel from Abigail and made it easy for him to repent when prophet Nathan rebuked him. Naaman exhibited a quality that many great and successful people may not possess. Just as Saul's servant pointed him in the direction of the prophet Samuel, Naaman's servants also pointed him to his healing.

Naaman was a great man but had leprosy. He had everything but still had a need that his money, connections, and status could not secure for him. I believe God has designed it such that no man can be complete, wanting nothing. It will only make you proud. Every human being will have to depend on somebody for something. In the real world, we often treat people who have not been so fortunate or blessed to be in our position like second-rate human beings.

First it was the little maid, the slave girl, who pointed Naaman to the source for healing for his leprosy (2 Kings 5: 2–4). When Naaman made it to Samaria, he almost returned to Syria because of his pride. His pride almost robbed him of his healing (5: 9–13). However, he shows an exemplary attitude of humility in listening to his servant's counsel. He later obeyed the prophet's instruction and was healed. How many of us have missed a blessing because we thought we knew better?

It is my sincere desire that God will turn your life around and clothe you with a spirit of humility and submissiveness so you can occupy your place. Do not allow your pride and arrogance to rob you of your deserved blessings. Pride is a quality of the devil. Do not follow the devil because you will also be cast out wherever you find yourself. The Lord is the God of second chances. I pray that every spirit of pride will be banished from your life. Ask the Lord to give you a humble spirit. He will give you a new heart if you ask.

Bad Attitude

A good attitude is always important in helping your development and hence promotion. No matter how gifted and talented you are, your rise to the top will remain stuck at a certain level if you have the wrong attitude. By attitude I am referring to how you conduct yourself in relation to the people around you. How do you relate to your boss, manager, supervisor, pastor, senior pastor, chief executive? What sort of attitude do you have towards those around you especially those who have authority over you? How do you react for example when you are offended by your superiors? What sort of body language do you display when you are asked to do something inconvenient?

How do you relate to people who you see as 'inferior' in intellect, status, or rank? How do you react when you are angry about something, or are placed under pressure at work, or are required to make certain sacrifices? What sort of attitude do you display when you cannot have your way, your opinion is rejected, or others appear not to like you? Do you moan, grumble, complain, murmur, and fight for your rights all the time? Or like the Bible stated, do you yield and wait for the right moment to resolve any grievance?

Many of us have missed out on becoming great because our attitude stank. We could not control our temper, that complaining attitude, and we essentially became difficult to work with. You need to understand that God will always use a person to promote you. God will rarely send an angel to push you along and mostly he will use people to accomplish his purposes. Even if God personally takes you to the top, you will still be dealing with human beings and must learn the art of relating to people.

Nobody succeeds in isolation. You always need people to either push you along or pull you through difficult times every step of the way. Thus, it pays to be nice to people on your way up, for those will be the same people you meet on the way down. As you reach the very top, the challenges will be great. You need people above you who can be your eyes and ears and be able to point you in the right direction. They must be able to freely direct, rebuke, correct, and instruct you without being afraid to do so. You also need people around you who you can trust and depend upon. You need all manner of people around you, great and small, because there is safety in numbers. "Where no counsel is, the people fall: but in the multitude of counsellors there is safety" (Proverbs 11: 14).

Nobody will invite a complainer into their midst because someone who has an awfully bad attitude is like a festering sore on the back of a wild animal. The quicker it heals, the better it is for the animal, because soon the vultures will start picking at it, and soon the animal's life, and possibly that of the whole group, will be at risk.

A person with a bad attitude is infectious, like "a little leaven that leaveneth the whole lump" (1 Corinthians 5: 6), because he or she would soon affect others and, with time, the whole group. It is why employees with bad attitude are hardly promoted or invited to drink tea or play golf with the boss. They are kept at a distance whilst those with a good attitude are promoted. If you have a bad attitude, change for the better.

The Key to Having the Right Attitude

A good attitude and the right attitude mixed with a good character will take you to greater heights. This is because those at the top will only extend a hand to pull you up to join them when they can trust you, depend on you, and feel you belong in the group. This has nothing to do with your gifts. It is a matter of people working together because they agree.

Of the twelve spies sent by Moses to the promised land (Numbers 13), ten had a bad attitude, and this would have affected the whole nation had it not been for the calming effect of the other two spies. Joshua and Caleb had a good attitude and supported the vision of the leader and therefore the agenda of God, who made the promise. Both had a certain commitment to the task assigned to them. They had a good attitude despite the fact there was opposition to the vision in the form of giants, hostile territories, and enemies. Is it any wonder that none of the murmurers and moaners inherited the Promised Land, except Joshua and Caleb? (Deuteronomy 1: 36–38)

You cannot control what people do or say to you, but you can control your own responses. "If the Spirit of the Ruler rises against thee do not leave your place, for yielding pacifieth great offences" (Ecclesiastes 10: 4).

A good attitude is important, in fact it is a very crucial factor in the rise and fall of many great and talented individuals. No one below you can promote you, only those above you can promote you. Always remember that.

Anyone desiring to get to the very top in their chosen profession will come against obstacles and opposition and may have to work under difficult circumstances. Sometimes you may have to work under different types of managers, supervisors, head pastors, and chief executives. Some may like you and some may loathe you for no apparent reason. Sometimes no matter what you do, it almost appears that those above you are never impressed. It almost feels as if all you get is destructive or negative feedback.

Many times, as you work your way to the top, you will be offended by many things. You will be provoked, frustrated, insulted, and abused, and it may even appear that your superiors have no faith in you. Just hold your peace and exhibit great character and attitude. Continue to work faithfully as if nothing has happened, and keep that enthusiasm going, and I can assure you that one day you will be rewarded with the promotion you so deserve. The Bible is so true that whenever you yield, offences are pacified.

Does that mean we should not complain when we are not being treated well? Should you allow yourself to be bullied, taken advantage of, or abused? Not at all. I am talking about how to respond when you have been rightfully offended. Sometimes, even when you are right, do not fight back and demand your rights or try to right the wrongs made against you. Ecclesiastes 10: 4 teaches us to learn to abide, persevere, and stay put even when we legitimately have a right to show resistance. Why? Because "a quiet spirit can overcome great mistakes" (NLT), and "composure and calmness prevent great offenses" (AMP).

You must always give thought to the consequences of your responses, actions, inactions, or overreactions because they can greatly affect your future. When you submit or yield, great offences will be resolved amicably in their own time. Proverbs 17: 28 says: "Even a fool who remains silent is considered wise, and the one who holds his tongue is deemed discerning".

Learn to respond wisely when provoked (Proverbs 15: 1). Learn to guard your heart with all the diligence you can find, otherwise your negative responses to provocations may destroy your future opportunities. You must learn how to hear and receive criticism without getting offended. Being overly sensitive and wearing your emotions on your sleeve only stop you from learning and stops those placed above you from training you. Learn when to respond, how to respond, what you must say, and why you must talk. The more you speak when emotional, the more likely you will say the wrong things (Proverbs 10: 19).

Why do most people react negatively to criticism? Is some criticism good for you? When you are confronted by what you perceive as enemies, what should your reaction be?

Whenever you are criticized or accused, there are always valuable lessons that can be learnt from the situation. Most of such incidents help us to develop character, resilience and prepare us for tougher times as we move up the promotion ladder.

David's refusal to kill Saul although he had a right to self-defence is a good attitude to follow. Again, David almost killed Nabal, were it not for the timely counsel of Abigail (1 Samuel 25: 32–33). You do not need to defend yourself all the time or plot revenge anytime someone offends you. Learn to stay calm.

Perhaps the reason you have not been promoted or received help from anyone is because of your poor attitude. Gifted as you may be, if you have a problem with attitude then doors of opportunity may continue to remain shut.

James 1: 19 admonishes: "Let everyone be quick to hear (be a careful, thoughtful listener), slow to speak (a speaker of carefully chosen words and), slow to anger (patient, reflective, forgiving)" (AMP).

"He who is slow to anger is better and more honourable than the mighty (soldier), and he who rules and controls his own spirit, than he who captures a city" (Proverbs 16: 3 AMP).

There is a great gift lying dormant in you that must be harnessed, but it may continue to lay fallow because of a poor attitude.

It is my prayer that you cultivate a sweet and excellent spirit. The sweet spirit that Caleb and Joshua possessed brought them promotion. The prophet Daniel had an excellent spirit. No wonder kings sought his counsel. Are you willing to cultivate this excellent spirit? It may be the missing factor to the breakthrough you have been waiting for.

Prayer: Lord grant me the strength to make the changes I need to make to develop an excellent spirit. You are the potter and I am the clay in your hands. Break me, mould me, fill me, and use me for your glory. In Jesus's name I pray.

4

Adversity and Trials: the Unseen
Catalyst to Your Greatness

Consider it nothing but joy, my brothers and sisters,
whenever you fall into various trials.

Be assured that the testing of your faith [through
experience] produces endurance [leading to spiritual
maturity, and inner peace]. And let endurance have
its perfect result and do a thorough work, so that you
may be perfect and completely developed [in your
faith], lacking in nothing.

—James 1: 2–4 AMP

"Success is to be measured not so much by the position one has
reached in life as by the obstacles which he has overcome while trying
to succeed"—Booker T. Washington

Trials come in different forms—afflictions, failures, adverse
situations, and many more. Nobody likes to go through difficult times.
No human being enjoys suffering. There is certainly no one who
would happily say that they would love to fail, suffer affliction, and go

through trials. Adam and Eve were cursed to a life of struggles, and as a result, we were all condemned to a life full of strife and suffering. But are adversities, failure, and afflictions necessarily a bad thing as we aim to make it to the top? Or are trials a necessary evil, the unseen catalyst to greatness?

Does failure mean that a person who is full of potential suddenly becomes devoid of it? Can a person who once was successful and has experienced setbacks recover and become successful again?

Trials, I have come to realise, have a lot of benefits and difficult times are like stepping stones to the very top. They form part of our success. I realise that trials can become the needed catalyst to set up a person.

"To err is human", so the adage goes. Anybody can fail and make mistakes, and we all have done so. Everybody at some point will face an adversity, a failure, and a challenging situation. God did not design for us not to go through adversity or make mistakes, as several scriptures confirm, but rather allows us to go through it to bring out the best in us. Every failure, mistake, or failed venture is an opportunity to learn, get better, go further, and rise higher.

Everyone has failed at something. You may have failed an exam, failed at a job interview, or failed at a business or relationship. I have failed exams before, both professional and non-professional. Every human being will at some point go through a difficult situation—a terminal illness, loss of a loved one, loss of a job, or loss of a business.

Beauty out of Ashes: My Personal Story

I too have failed a fair few times in life. I wish I could say my life has been devoid of trials, challenges, and failed ventures. Far from it. I would not even qualify to write this chapter if I had never experienced adversity. I know what it means to suffer loss, financially or otherwise, how it feels to fail an exam, not once but a few times, and what it means to be rejected, dejected, and unappreciated. I have been there.

But through it all, I now, more than most, understand that truly "all things work together for good". I now hugely appreciate James 1: 2–4.

I mentioned earlier that I did not do well in my GCSE. I failed at the first attempt, to put it mildly. I also failed a pathology exam whilst in medical school, failed a professional paediatric exam in the United Kingdom, and failed an initial attempt at my professional membership exams. I also failed at a few relationships before I met my wife. I failed my driving theory test a whopping three times before passing. So, as you can see, I have earned some stripes.

Those setbacks, however, did not prevent nor discourage me from attempting further exams or entering a new relationship. I wish my life were perfect, but it is not. Do I have any regrets? No, because I am a work in progress. I know the Lord is working something incredibly beautiful with my life (Job 23: 10). The fact I am even sharing this testimony to encourage someone else tells me that sometimes setbacks happen for a reason. The Lord will use your personal story as a testimony to strengthen others, so do not give up (Luke 22: 23–25).

Following my first GCSE, I travelled to the United Kingdom to visit my parents for holidays whilst waiting for my results. When the results were released, my dad was rightly disappointed. I returned to Ghana after my holidays with the view of starting all over again. For the next three years, I was not in formal education, not in any apprenticeship, and not in work. There was no hope, no future, no sense of direction at all. I was forlorn, disappointed with myself. I later settled down to an uncertain future, going through the daily motions with my friends, most of whom were in the same situation as I was. I had no vision of my present state and never once imagined being who I am today. And I believe strongly that as long as you hold on to your faith in God and believe that our thoughts are not God's thoughts and our ways are not God's ways, then one day there will be light at the end of that tunnel.

Speak to great achievers, and many will tell you that the setbacks and failures they experienced defined their lives or made them successful. It helped them develop character and resilience, which defined their lives. Many great people we read about failed many times before they eventually made it. Many faced different adversities before achieving ultimate success. Their lives inspire us. There are also many rags-to-riches stories and many scientific breakthroughs or inventions that were a result of failed or botched experiments.

It is interesting to note that Sir Alex Ferguson—the most successful football manager in British soccer history—was just one game away from being sacked as manager of Manchester United. The rest, they say, is history. There is a thin line between success and failure, so do not be too hard on yourself if you go through difficulty.

"Many of life's failures are people who did not realise how close they were to success when they gave up"—Thomas Edison

The fact that you have failed at a business, at an examination, or at a job interview does not mean that suddenly you become a bad businessperson or bad employee or bad human being. Talent will always be permanent, so when you have a setback, remember that you can always start over again. Class is always permanent, but form can be temporary. A setback does not mean that you have suddenly become a failure at the very thing you succeeded in before. Failing an exam certainly does not mean you cannot pass it if you correct your mistakes and give it another try.

Sometimes a kick in the backside is what one needs to get going. The apostles were getting too comfortable in Jerusalem after Christ's death, and had it not been for persecution, the great commission may never have been fulfilled.

"Our greatest weakness lies in giving up. The most certain way to succeed is always to try one more time"—Thomas Edison

Without the lessons that are learnt from setbacks, you cannot survive at the very top level. The higher you rise the tougher it becomes, and the greater the opposition can be. As you work your way to the top, be prepared to be tested, grilled, and toughened by the lessons learnt from adversity. Pure gold is only obtained through a process of purification.

I mentioned Sir Isaac Newton at the beginning of the book. He used to be at the bottom of his class in every subject. A boy in his class was always at the top of every subject. This boy used to constantly taunt him, calling him stupid and useless. Newton states that he only took an interest in his schoolwork after he was involved in *a* fight with this boy. It changed his life. He'd had enough of the taunting and decided to fight back. He fought this boy and inflicted a bloody nose and bruised cheek. His classmates hailed Newton as a champion. This physical victory spurred him on, and he decided to prove this boy wrong once and for all by beating him academically as well. From that moment, Newton says he studied hard, and before the end of that school year, he was top in nearly every subject.

Assuming this boy had not been Newton's nemesis, the world would have lost out big time on such a genius. Supposing he had not decided to face his fears and prove this boy wrong, he would never have known how great he was destined to be. It goes without saying that it is better to try and fail than not to try at all.

Trials Bring out the Best in You

"But he knows the way that I take (and he pays attention to it): when he has tried me, I will come forth as (refined) gold (pure and luminous)" (Job 23: 10 AMP).

I believe many tea lovers have made the same observation as I have: you only get a good quality flavoured tea if the water you are using has boiled properly. Once upon a time, I was desperate for a cup of tea, and because I could not wait to put the kettle on, I decided to use the water left over in the flask. This water was several hours old and not quite hot, just lukewarm. It still managed to extract some flavour from the tea bag, but the tea was hopelessly odourless and tasteless. However, when I used water boiled at one hundred degrees Celsius (212 Fahrenheit), it was able to extract all the excellent flavours locked up in the teabag, resulting in an excellent brew. It suddenly dawned on me that water must boil to a certain temperature to bring out the flavour locked in the teabag.

In much the same way, we need to go through the same purifying process. Pure gold is only obtained when it is refined through fire. God has designed that we go through trials to become better (Isaiah 48: 10–11). God does this for his own glory. He could have spared you. After all, it takes more heat to purify gold than it does for silver. Are you seeking to be like gold or silver?

I heard the lyrics to the song "Stronger" by Kelly Clarkson: "What doesn't kill you makes you stronger, stand a little taller", and I thought about how vaccines protect us from deadly diseases. They are sometimes painful to receive but necessary.

Some live vaccines are made with what is called attenuated viruses, where it is not completely dead but deactivated to stimulate the body's immune system. In rare cases it may simulate the actual disease it is meant to prevent, but generally it makes you stronger. It is the same principle with trials. They are not designed to kill you but to make you stronger.

God did not remove David, Daniel, Shadrach, Meshach, Abednego, or Paul from the line of fire. And Jesus did not prevent Peter from being 'sifted like wheat' by Satan. He glorified himself through their afflictions. Daniel was left in the den with the lions, Israel walked through the wilderness for forty years, and the thorn was not removed from Paul's flesh. David had to battle Goliath and then one adversity after another before and during his kingship. One thing was clear—God was with them all the way. He will be with you too.

We live in an overly critical world where every slip is magnified as a failing. People are no longer supportive and compassionate, and our critics are eager to 'crucify' us and finish us off. Success comes at a price. Do you know that before one vaccine or drug is developed, it costs millions of pounds and sometimes many botched experiments to successfully produce? Sometimes the whole experiment is discontinued despite the vast amount of money that had been invested in it.

"Do not judge me by my successes, judge me by how many times I fell down and got back up again"—Nelson Mandela

Have you observed a toddler learning how to walk? They wobble around objects, walking unsteadily and falling many times. Each time, after crying a little when they get hurt, they are up again toddling. Toddlers rarely stay stuck to the floor once they discover the adventure of walking. Through the falls, bruises, and tears, learning how to walk becomes an adventure until they start walking. And then they start running. Perfection comes after they have failed many times. Initial trepidation gives way to confidence, and with confidence comes expression of potential.

It is the same with our lives. Each day is an adventure, and the lessons learnt from failure must spur us on to achieving better things and soaring to greater heights.

It should be how we treat adversity. Problems will always come into our lives. There will always be situations that can make us depressed, stressed, disgusted, and busted. How you handle that situation will determine whether you remain on the floor forever or get up and continue. Sadly, many people like to throw a 'pity party' when adversity strikes.

Since adversities are part of life and cannot be avoided, we must learn to embrace them without fear. The best approach will be to analyse the bad situation you find yourself in, correct what can be corrected, learn what be learnt, and apply any lessons from that situation to make you better. There have been so many zero-to-hero, ashes-to-glory, or rags-to-riches stories. We are surrounded by many successful people whose lives should inspire us not to give up easily. There is always a blessing in that bad situation because all things work together for good. Obstacles in your life can become stepping stones to future success (Romans 8: 28).

Joseph believed he was destined for greatness. But the door to that greatness was not via preparatory school, grammar school, or an Ivy League university. The door to his greatness lay in serving Midianites, serving in Potiphar's house (as senior housekeeper), and then serving in prison (as senior prisoner overseer). From one form of servitude to another, Joseph never imagined that the suffering he was going through, losing his personal freedom, and going through hardship was designed to teach him leadership and stewardship. It was in Potiphar's house and in prison that he acquired the skills of stewardship. In both places he learnt to govern and oversee things and manage people on a smaller scale. It was tough, and sometimes it was depressing, and it was not the vision he had for himself—certainly not the future he envisaged when he dreamt.

But the Lord was preparing him to govern on a larger scale and for future leadership. After he interpreted Pharaoh's dream, Pharaoh told Joseph he was the best man for the role (Genesis 41: 37–43).

The suffering he endured, the difficulties and lessons learnt serving as a slave and a prisoner became stepping stones to greatness. I do not know what you have been through or what you have had to endure, but do not despise the trials that have come your way. The door to your palace may not look glistening but if you have wisdom you will understand all things work together for good.

The grace bestowed on his life (dreaming and interpreting dreams) was still present (Romans 11: 29), but God needed to prepare him to occupy his rightful place. I see your affliction being turned around for good, a garment of praise for the spirit of heaviness and beauty for ashes. The Lord will fulfil his word concerning your life in Jesus's name.

> Every detail works to your advantage and to God's glory.... So we're not giving up. How could we! Even though on the outside it often looks like things are falling apart on us, on the inside, where God is making new life, not a day goes by without his unfolding grace. These hard times are like small potatoes compared to the coming good times, the lavish celebration prepared for us. There's far more here than meets the eye. The things we see now are here today, gone tomorrow. But the things we can't

see now will last forever. (2 Corinthians 4: 15–18 The Message)

Men put a thief on the cross to die for his sins, but Jesus did not think twice about what it was he had done and straightway took him to paradise. Never be afraid to make a mistake or fail at anything because perfection only comes with practice, and in practice we will fail sometimes. It is important that when you have tried and failed, find someone who can show you love and compassion, put an arm around you, and encourage you to try again.

If you find yourself at this crossroads, I need you to believe that God has not forgotten you. Do not perceive the difficulties you are facing now as the final straw and throw in the towel. Hold on, because one of these days that knock on your door will show you deliverance and promotion. You must change your perception of failure and use every challenge as an opportunity to grow and improve.

Take Responsibility for Your Own Actions

You are responsible for your own life. Do not blame what could have happened. Accept your faults, take an introspective look at where you went wrong, correct your mistakes, and become better next time. It cannot always be someone else's fault. It is not possible that everyone else is always wrong except you.

It is so easy to point the finger of blame at someone for your woes. It is true that what happens to us is greatly influenced by the world around us. Ultimately, however, the sum effect of where you are in life depends on one person—you.

Perhaps you never had a father or mother in your life, nor were you born into a rich home or had a rich benefactor. Maybe you were born in a village or did not get a good education. The question is: What can you do about that unfortunate circumstance?

Some circumstances you can change and others you can do

nothing about. In most cases, search for the divine strength to move on when the unfortunate happens.

Maybe the serenity prayer can help you: "God, grant me the courage to change the things I can, the serenity to accept the things I cannot change, and the wisdom to know the difference".

If you can allow that to sink into your spirit and let the past go so you can focus on the future, then you are already halfway on the road to succeeding. If you hold on to the past, you get stuck and cannot move on. Release your grip on the past and stride into the future with glorious hope. The future always holds hope for those who are prepared to face it.

The Key to Learning from Mistakes and Failures

Learning from your own mistakes takes boldness and courage because most of us go on the defensive when we make a mistake. It is only the proud and arrogant who find it difficult to admit they are wrong or have made a mistake.

Do not be ashamed to admit you have made a mistake. Anyone who finds it difficult to admit will have to live a life of lies. Such people keep creating a facade until the web of lies gradually entangles and destroys them. Some people feel that an admission of failure means you become less of a human being. There is nothing shameful about making a mistake; we all do so. Show me any great person who has never made a mistake, and I will show you an alien from another planet.

First you must be honest enough to admit that you have made a mistake. Then you feel free mentally to seek solutions—and then restoration occurs. An admission of failure takes great courage; it is a sign of maturity. Acknowledging you are wrong is usually the first step to restoration.

The problem Cain had was blaming his brother, Abel, when God rejected his offering of the fruit of the land. Cain failed to realize that his attitude towards the sacrifice he was presenting was wrong.

He most likely approached it anyhow and did not accord God the reverence he deserved. Like Esau, he did not value spiritual things. It was why his sacrifice was rejected. I believe it had nothing to do with the fruit of the ground—he was a tiller of the ground and brought produce from the work of his hands. It was possibly his whole attitude and how he presented his offering.

Abel, on the other hand, revered God, took the exercise seriously, and made a better presentation. His offering of the firstborn of his flock was respected by God.

Cain's killing of Abel was out of envy. He could have admitted he was wrong, and God would have forgiven him. His unrepentant attitude resulted in murder.

Saul blamed his disobedience to a simple instruction on the pressure of the people. If he had admitted his mistakes, he and his descendants would have possibly continued to rule. He blamed others for his failure to provide strong leadership (1 Samuel 15: 10-28). He apologized rather belatedly after he was rejected by God, but by then it was too late to salvage his kingship.

David, on the other hand, immediately apologized to prophet Nathan as soon as his crime was revealed to him. Whilst he still suffered the consequences of his actions, he earned a reprieve from God. He kept his kingship and was still called a friend of God. He was a man who understood what it meant to be humble and have a contrite heart.

Once a mistake has been made, the next crucial step is to analyse the situation and learn what went wrong and what went right. Learn from any positives that came out of the situation, review the mistakes that were made, learn from them, and become a better person.

Three important things happened to the prodigal son and led to his redemption. He realised he was wrong; he made a U-turn and went back to seek help at his father's house, and he acknowledged to his father that he made a mistake. He did not feel too big to apologise. He received a reprieve and restoration.

Learn from Other People's Mistakes

> I went past the field of the slothful, and by the
> vineyard of the man void of understanding; and, lo,
> it was all grown over with thorns, and nettles had
> covered the face thereof, and the stone wall thereof
> was broken down. Then I saw, and considered it
> well: I looked upon it, and received instruction. Yet
> a little sleep, a little slumber, a little folding of the
> hands to sleep: so shall thy poverty come as one that
> travelleth; and thy want as an armed man. (Proverbs
> 24: 30–34)

"Go to the ant, thou sluggard; consider her ways, and be wise"
(Proverbs 6: 6).

To *consider* something means "to think about carefully especially
regarding taking some action; to gaze on steadily and reflectively"
(Merriam-Webster Dictionary).

To receive instruction means the situation will impart some
lessons to you and help you make changes to your own life for the
better. In this scripture, Solomon was saying that he observed a lazy
man and learnt a lesson: that if are lazy and do not work on your
gifts or talents or do not take good care of what you have, you will
eventually become poor. Indeed, too much sleep leads to poverty.

Solomon demonstrates that when you see a situation, whether
positive or negative, observe it closely, reflect on it, and learn lessons
from it. Reflection is an effective way to move forward in life. If
someone you know is doing well in life, there are aspects of his or her
life you can observe and possibly implement to make yourself better.
If someone's ministry is thriving, his or her business is booming, or
this person is doing better academically than you are, you can always
consider it, receive instruction, and become better.

The ability to stay still and observe is a skill that one must develop.

Several times in the Bible, God instructs us to observe something diligently. This means it is not easy to keep still, pay attention to something, and draw lessons. God understands how unsettled we can become and how easily we get distracted. He told Joshua, "Meditate therein day and night, that thou mayest observe to do according to all that is written therein" (Joshua 1: 8). This means that if Joshua did not always pay careful attention and remain diligent, he was unlikely to follow the instructions, and the result would be failure.

Every situation we face can teach us something. Instructions come to us daily, either directly and indirectly, sometimes in plain language and sometimes indirectly. Sometimes they are easy to understand, but many times you need an ability to discern or perceive what something means. Everything you see, hear, or experience will teach you something and impact you either positively or negatively. Whether it was your mistake or someone else's, there are always lessons to be learnt. Failure to learn from mistakes leads to a cycle of repeated mistakes.

You go through tests that teach you lessons in life, but in school you are taught a lesson before being tested. Do you see the difference?

You must develop the ability to draw understanding from the things you see and hear so that you do not miss the lessons you are meant to learn. If you can learn to do that, you may be on your way to breaking out and moving forward.

Find Strength in Victories

Make every effort to put the past behind you and remember the victories you have had. David remembered how he killed a bear and a lion with his own hands, and this encouraged him to overcome a bigger challenge in Goliath. I knew I was good enough to pass the GCSE and other exams I had failed if I applied myself diligently. Each time, I learnt from my mistakes and succeeded.

Remember the good times. Dwell on your strengths and not your failures. Positive thinking is vital. Every little victory is meant for a purpose, to spur us on to greater victories. If today you have been able to gather ten people in your little church, learn from the positive things you did, correct the mistakes you made to improve things, and by God's grace your church may surely grow. Do not despise small beginnings or small victories (Job 8: 7).

In Joshua 14: 7–12, we see another example of a man (Caleb) who, at age 85, was prepared to take on new challenges by recalling the victories that God had given him when he was younger. In Judges 16: 28–29, Samson cries out to God to strengthen him one last time. He remembered victories he'd had with God's help.

Small beginnings should always lead to great endings if you are willing to learn from past mistakes. Trust in the lord that every situation you have faced can become a stepping stone to greater victory. In Jesus's name. Amen.

Where Do You Find Your Source of Strength in Times of Difficulty?

Who and where do you go to when faced with adversity? Do you surround yourself with people who can give you timely, wise, biblical counsel that brings restoration to your soul? Or like many, do you prefer to surround yourself with people who will make the situation worse?

It is important to seek out those who can strengthen and encourage you with words that will soothe your suffering and lessen your anguish (Job 16: 1–5). I was fortunate enough to get timely counsel as I struggled through three years of my life without purpose. After struggling after my GCSE failure, my breakthrough came in the form of timely counsel from two women: a schoolmate's mum, and my deceased paternal grandmother.

I had known my friend's mum since our secondary school days and had kept in touch. We lived in different towns, but anytime I travelled through their town, I visited their store at the marketplace to say hello to the parents and see my friend. On one occasion, his mum had a discussion with me about my future, and through her encouragement and counsel I felt positive about myself and left with a real sense of purpose and determination that I could do the things she said I could.

Within the same month, I visited my paternal grandmother, who was then completely blind. Interestingly, she gave me similar counsel and encouragement to what my friend's mum gave me. I am without doubt that this timely counsel set me on course to where I find myself today.

I started implementing the advice they gave me, and by the grace of God my situation improved. It is true that with the aged is wisdom (Job 12: 12), and in the multitude of counsel, purposes are established.

The counsel you receive in time of crisis can either make or break you, so surround yourself with people who are more likely to encourage you. Find the right people in your moments of difficulty. Proverbs 25: 11 says, "A word fitly spoken is like apples of gold in pictures of silver".

Again, we learn that, "A man hath joy by the answer of his mouth: and a word spoken in season, how good is it" (Proverbs 15: 23).

It is so vital to know who you lean on in times of adversity. Surround yourself with those who can give you godly counsel, not people who will make the situation worse by judging or condemning you. Instead speak to those who can constructively point out your mistakes to you, help you to see the positives you can take out of the situation, help you to correct the mistakes you have made and strengthen you for the future using God's word.

Never Stop Believing in Yourself in Difficult Times

When adversity strikes, never stop believing in who you are, and do not doubt your inner strength. Do not forget victories and things you did so well in times past. Many of us are not aware of how resilient we are until pushed to the limits. It is what tests your innate abilities. When you must go through difficult times, never lose sight of the fact that you have had victories before. Your sense of failure or success should not depend on the opinion of a man but on God's opinion of you. You must not see yourself as a failure because someone says or thinks so. Your sense of success or failure will depend on the mentality you adopt—whether as a giant-slayer or a grasshopper.

Your future greatness does not depend on your personal or present difficult circumstances. Greater things are yet to come. Learn to encourage yourself in the Lord. David trusted in how God made him and his 'personal armour' (1 Samuel 17: 38–40). David found strength in the word of God.

God Will Be with You through the Trials

God did not promise that we will never be tried (Isaiah 43: 1–3), but he promised that he will be with us when we faced challenges. That for sure is a promise—as sure as his word 'which will accomplish every purpose it was sent for'. God watches over his word to perform it. You can be sure that he will not always take you out of the trial, but he will eventually grant you a way of escape.

The good news is that adversities do not remain forever. They are limited. There is always victory ahead of us. Your 'morning' is coming, and your joy will be full. Hold on, and do not give up yet, for your victory is on the way.

I pray that you develop unflinching faith and trust in God. Your storm will soon be over. Amen.

5

The Secret Key to Tarrying

"But let endurance and steadfastness and patience
have full play and do a thorough work, so that you
may be (people) perfectly and fully developed (with
no defects), lacking in nothing" (James 1: 4 AMP).

This scripture from the book of James makes it clear that on your
way to the top you will face several different types of obstacles. These
obstacles are unavoidable, and possibly allowed by God, to help equip
you for the task ahead. They are designed to build an especially
important quality you need—patience.

Why is patience such an essential quality—it is because *between*
the period when a seed is sown, when investments have been made
and the harvest is something called *time*. During the intervening
period between 'planting and harvest', the seed would need to go
through a process to turn it into the right product. If you speed up this
process, for example through artificial ripening, the taste of the fruit
is completely different from the naturally ripened fruit.

Chicken raised the natural way always taste better (in my humble
opinion) than that raised by genetic engineering, and naturally grown

oranges have a better aromatic smell and taste than that grown genetically.

Patience Lays the Foundation for Future Success

"He is like a man which built an house, and digged deep, and laid the foundation on a rock: and when the flood arose, the stream beat vehemently upon that house, and could not shake it: for it was founded upon a rock" Luke 6: 48).

"If the foundation be destroyed, what can the righteous do?" (Psalm 11: 3)

Foundations take time; the deeper they are, the taller the building. Trees with deep roots, like the palm, the cedar of Lebanon, and the baobab withstand drought better than those with shallow roots. This is because such trees can draw water from deep water tables underneath the earth.

I was in Dubai a few years ago and visited the Burj Khalifa, the world's tallest building. This amazing building is founded on a very solid foundation, and without this foundation the building would collapse. I stood by one of the new buildings in its foundational stages and it was incredible how much steel and concrete was being used to reinforce them.

Patience, like a good foundation, enables a child of God to be fully prepared for success at the very top. It lays the foundation upon which future success is built. What you may not appreciate is that every experience you have been through until this point is designed to make you better. All things work together for your good. God makes all things beautiful in his own time. Your preparation may take any number of years. That is why you must develop this great quality called patience. Because if you do not, you may be destroyed before your harvest season arrives.

If your preparation is not right, you will struggle for the rest of your life. Ecclesiastes 10: 10 - (KJV) states that "If the iron (axe in some versions) be blunt, and he do not whet the edge, then must he put to more strength: but wisdom is profitable to direct'.

If you are going to cut down a tough tree, you must first spend time sharpening your axe. If you do not and start straightaway, you will have to spend more time and apply more energy to cut that tree. Using a sharp axe takes less time than cutting a tree with a blunt axe. For with a sharp axe, you can cut down the tree quite smoothly and quickly without using much physical strength. A sharp axe will save you using a great deal of strength and wasting time. In the same way without patient preparation, you may make unfortunate mistakes in life that could significantly impact your ability to break forth and make progress.

Let me use the illustration of a newborn human. When a baby is born, it is initially dependent on its parents for everything. During the first few months, a baby can neither walk nor run. As the months pass, the neck strengthens, the baby is able to roll over, and by six months it may be able to sit. Its muscles gradually develop, tone improves, and the baby then starts to pull up in order to stand, toddle around furniture, and then takes its first steps independently. In time, it walks with confidence and finally can run. God designed its development in a specific way. Every stage is programmed, and the baby spends time in each developmental stage to learn, make mistakes, have a few falls, gain confidence, and then move to the next level for a new test.

If the baby's motor development does not follow the sequential developmental pattern, there will be problems. Just imagine a 6-month-old trying to run when it cannot walk. It is the same principle God applies to our lives when he is taking us to higher heights.

It is wise to learn to tarry as you work towards your success. You cannot grasp the learning at university level when you enter straight from primary school, no matter how clever you are as a child. Do not be in a hurry to get to the very top before you are ready.

I shared the story of Joseph earlier. He was a dreamer and strongly believed this dream would be fulfilled but was not aware of the obstacles he would face first. He did not yet understand the significance of that dream. He needed to be prepared physically, emotionally, mentally, and psychologically to stand in the office God was preparing him for. He needed to go through the wilderness experience, get thrown into prison and experience the frustration and disappointment of ungrateful people. He was betrayed by his brothers, sold into slavery, worked as a servant, and spent time in prison before becoming a prime minister.

God had to work on Joseph's character through the experiences he went through before his promotion. Joseph had the patience to wait for his harvest (his crowning as a prime minister). He allowed God to work on his character through diverse ways and by the time God had finished with him, he was a solid, god-fearing, faithful man full of integrity. His godly character and the fear of God's word preserved him until his promotion.

His period of preparation took almost thirteen years between the time he was sold into slavery (Genesis 37: 2) and his coronation as a prime minister. The experiences he went through steeled him for the pressures at the top and this is what many who are in a hurry to reach the top do not envisage. There is a price to pay to get to the top and especially, to remain at the top. The responsibilities of leadership and stewardship can be incredibly challenging, and if you are not well equipped to handle the pressure, it will destroy you. Hasty climbers, it must be said, are more likely to have a sudden fall.

Moses needed to be prepared for his task ahead. His God-given role on earth was to lead an entire nation out of a foreign land, change their slavery mentality, and get them to have a relationship with a God they were not familiar with whilst living in Egypt. This was no mean feat. As the leader of a new nation yet to be created, he needed to be prepared not just to lead but taught how to rule. He also needed to be taught how to serve in humility.

The first part of his life was spent in the palace learning about leadership, royalty, and ruling. The next phase was spent in the wilderness, in a strange land. He had to be taught how to abound and abase, because life is not always smooth sailing. He learnt to be content (Exodus 2: 21) living in those conditions, which were completely different from royalty. He needed to understand the natural condition of the group he was going to lead. Without that, he might even struggle to exhibit any empathy or compassion for those he would lead. We see many leaders today who do not care about the welfare of those they oversee. To them, people are just numbers, a tool to accomplish their vision, a means to justify their end goals.

Years later, when Moses returned to negotiate with Pharaoh, you could see he was not intimidated because he was used to observing court. He had been educated as a royal child and could conduct himself and speak like one. He knew what to say, how to say it, and when to say it. He was the king's adopted son. When he came back to stand before Pharaoh, he was 80, having spent forty years in the palace and then another forty in the wilderness. He spent the remaining forty years of his life leading and ruling. He spent his first eighty years being prepared to fulfil his God-given purpose in the last forty years of his life. He died at the age of 120. I do not know how many of us are willing to wait for eighty years to be trained for our assignments.

David had been earmarked for kingship, but again, his journey to the top was not to be smooth. He needed to be prepared to survive at the very top. The first part of his life was spent as a shepherd and learning how to serve. The wilderness was where he honed his fighting skills and playing the harp. He needed to be prepared for the battle against Goliath by having battles with lions and bears.

The next phase of his life was spent in the palace. In his wisdom, God knew that David had to learn about royalty and kingship and planned it such that he would obtain an education. He completed his training as a guerrilla fighter, moving from place to place, always on the run and experiencing the highs and lows of life. He was crowned king at age 30 with at least fifteen years of hard training behind him.

David had the courage and character to wait for God's appointed time to be the next king of Israel. He had several opportunities to kill Saul and prematurely rule the kingdom of Israel. David had already been anointed by Samuel and knew that God would fulfil his promise.

But he was also very spiritual to understand the importance of times and seasons and allowing the move of God at the right time. Even when he had the opportunity to kill Saul and pressure was put on him by his friends (who quoted scripture to back their encouragement), he was wise enough not to touch God's anointed (1 Samuel 24: 5–6). His godly patience meant he was not desperate to become king and thus never rebelled.

When you read about David, you realize he was a young man who knew and feared God. That fear and respect for the things of God governed his attitude and conduct in everything (save the matter of Bathsheba and Uriah the Hittite).

He was a young king but a very rugged and experienced young man who was skilled at serving, leading, judging, and mingling with royalty. He was also skilled in warfare because part of his assignment was to fight and secure the borders of the land God was giving to Israel. You may recollect that when he tried to build a tabernacle for the Lord, it was made clear to him this was not his assignment. He was equipped for the purpose he had been created to fulfil.

I am sharing this for you to understand that every season of your life so far has been designed by God to bring you to an expected end. Allow God to finish his work in you, and do not be in a hurry to hasten the process. Joseph, Moses, David, and even Daniel had to be prepared for the very top. You will not be any different as a child of God, so have the patience to wait for your time. Do not be in a hurry. Let the Refiner finish his work in you, and at the right time he will make all things beautiful.

"To everything there is a season, and a time to every purpose under the heaven" (Ecclesiastes 3: 1—2).

The Benefits of Tarrying until the Dream Is Fulfilled

Stay at one place until you flourish. Stay with one vision until it is accomplished. Permanence is an important quality to adopt if you are to flourish. It is a mark of good decision making. The conditions at present may not be conducive but stay put. The ability to stay put and complete your training or apprenticeship sometimes under the most testing of circumstances requires a lot of divine wisdom. A lack of godly counsel has resulted in many a talented individual pressing the self-destruct button. You do not bear fruit at the right time because you keep moving from job to job or church to church prematurely either because of your bad attitude, temperament, or lack of maturity. Understand that sometimes under very testing circumstances you must still abide.

The ability to abide and remain at one place for a long time has its own rewards. Stability brings rewards—people that are usually promoted from within to manage large companies have usually been around a long time. They have been tested over a long period of time, trusted, and been found dependable. Over a long period they would have experienced the ups and downs of the company and understand its vision, mission, and ethics. Most of these people will tell you that it had not always been rosy working there, but they learnt to stay put despite testing circumstances. That sort of attitude has its own blessings.

"Be patient therefore, brethren, unto the coming of the lord. Behold, the husbandman waiteth for the precious fruit of the earth, and hath long patience for it, until he receive the early and latter rain" (James 5: 7).

After we have discovered our gifts, invested in our potential, and done all that is required of us to succeed, how willing are we to wait for the harvest? Many of us are in a hurry to reap our harvest after we have planted. Let us bear in mind what the Bible says about seasons, harvest, waiting, and the timing of things. We are so impatient to be like other people that we will do anything to get to the top quickly.

"Then I will give you rain in their season, and the land will yield her produce and the trees of the field bear their fruit" (Leviticus 26: 4 - amp).

"That He will give the rain for your land in its season, the early [fall] and late [spring] rain, so that you may gather in your grain and your new wine and your [olive] oil" (Deuteronomy 11: 14 - amp).

When you have tarried and allowed God to bring about your increase at the right time, you tend to have good and longer-lasting success. There is always the danger, in this present world, of allowing the trappings of other people's success get to you. Riches and success attract power, prestige, and adulation, and these are difficult to resist. We love comparing ourselves to others, bringing untold pressure on ourselves (2 Corinthians 10: 12). Pressure comes in many forms: from family and friends, as well as enemies.

You see when you put different seeds into the same fertile soil with the same conditions, they do not all germinate (shoot up from the ground) at the same time. Each seed is different in its make-up. Whilst some seeds quickly germinate within days (for example, beans and corn plants) others (for example, the palm and coconut trees) need to absorb a lot of moisture and other special factors before they can shoot up.

However, it is interesting to note that the plants that are the fastest to shoot up and bear fruits early also do die off quicker. They tend not to be evergreen. They tend to be seasonal. Their lives are shorter and can only bear a certain minimum amount of fruit. On the other hand, the plants that are slow growing like the palm, coconut, cedar, or baobab trees tend to go on forever, bearing fruits season after season. This highlights the importance of laying solid foundations and preparation and of apprenticeships on your way to breaking forth. You need it for long-lasting success.

I believe that Sarah, Rachel, Hannah, and Elizabeth were made barren for a good reason. God was not unreasonable in delaying their fruitfulness. They may not have understood the bigger picture initially, but God withheld their ability to have children because the fruits coming out of the womb of these faithful Christian sisters were special. Isaac, Joseph, Samuel, and John the Baptist were all born for a special purpose. God had to prepare their parents for these special assignments.

So if you have not yet had your breakthrough, and if your vision has tarried for a little while, I encourage you to keep trusting and waiting because he who promises is faithful (Hebrews 10: 22–24). I pray that you will allow the word of God to abide in you and wait patiently for your breakthrough.

May you fulfil your gifts at the right time, may your vines never cast her fruit before their time in the field (Malachi 3: 11), and may you reap the right harvest at the right time in the right season.

6

It All Begins with a Vision

And the Lord answered me, and said, Write the Vision, and make it plain upon tables, that he may run that readeth it. For the vision is yet for an appointed time.

—Habakkuk 2: 2–3

Your Vision Makes You

The Advanced English Dictionary & Thesaurus defines vision as "the formation of a mental image of something that is not perceived as real and is not present to the senses". This means you have a picture in your mind of what you want your future to be. It is personal and unique to you. It is what you 'see' that others cannot see or understand.

God is the originator of visions and He gives us visions that lead to great accomplishments. Whether or not the person is a believer, great visions are always from God. He is the one who created you and placed in you the innate ability to succeed. He has already made grace and provision for your vision to succeed.

Vision is not the same as sight. The Advanced English Dictionary defines sight as "the ability to see". Even though we talk about testing your vision this refers to sight when you go to see an optician. Vision has a deeper meaning than sight. Vision is related to perception. Vision has something to do with thinking. Perception has to do with the use of the mind. I believe that having a vision is a spiritual function and it is God that activates this spiritual function in every person.

The use of your mind is particularly important in formulating your vision because inventions and achievements do not just happen. There is a clear distinction between physically looking at something with your eyes and having perception about something. Whereas looking means seeing something that is physically tangible or can be touched, seeing in that statement refers to perception, which is essentially a function of the mind. Therefore, vision is more related to the mind and thinking.

Let me give you an example. You can walk into a community centre and see a group of people present every day and just see them as users of the facility. Another person will see the same group in that same community centre and perceive they will be hungry and thirsty after being at the centre. This will then generate a corner shop or business on the premises. That is perception at work.

The starting point of any endeavour is vision. Nothing takes shape if first it has not been thought through. Before a building is built the owner already has a vision of what they want to accomplish. He then gets an architect or building engineer to put those thoughts on paper (building plan or drawing) before the project eventually takes off.

It is why vision is described as a function of the heart—because it has moved from the mind and has now entered your heart (your spirit realm), without which the vision does not become all—consuming. Once it enters the heart, the individual then channels his or her energy into pursuing this dream or vision. "Where there is no vision, people perish" (Proverbs 29: 18).

The Bible says that in the beginning, God created the heavens and the earth. This means he thought about what he was about to do, a vision about what he wanted to accomplish. For example, when he had a vision to create man, he already knew how man was going to be fruitful without God repeatedly making new babies every day. Therefore, for every living creature or living thing, there is a mechanism to produce after their kind. It is called genetics. In simple terms, God had a vision.

Without a vision, you cannot even start to maximise your potential. The human being is beautifully and wonderfully crafted. God made man in his own image, and since God is creative, man is expected to be creative. In the absence of an illness that affects the brain or thinking ability, every man is uniquely created by God to fulfil a role on earth. Each creation has a specific assignment to make it a better place for the rest of humankind.

You need to have an idea what you want to do in the future or a thought what you want to accomplish. Once you have that vision, you can set about accomplishing it. If there is no vision, your life may end up nowhere.

Decide what you want to do in the future if you are young. Your life is not some lottery. Do not leave it to chance. There is an idea waiting to be birthed, a vision waiting to be accomplished, and an invention waiting to be created, lying dormant in your mind.

I had my university education in a part of Ghana called Kumasi. In that region, the indigenous people are very business-minded and progressive. I realised that people from that part of the country were used to building houses and owning businesses, and they commonly spoke about the houses they owned or were building, the cars they owned, the lands they possessed, and the businesses they owned. It did not matter how young they were, they seemed to have a vision about what they wanted to do in the future. The vision to own a house for example, gave them a sense of purpose to work. As soon as somebody has a purpose to build a house or own their own home, they do not waste money. In this environment, I learnt that it was easy to build a house. It enabled them to use money wisely. They became productive and creative as a result because there was an end goal.

Once you have it in your heart that this is what you want to do, you channel your mind, energy, resources, and creativity to accomplishing this vision. Without a vision, you will perish, and you may end up nowhere in life, stagnant and blaming everyone.

Three Things to Do When Formulating a Vision

1. Spend Time Praying about What You Want to Accomplish

"I will stand upon my watch, and set me upon the tower, and will watch to see what he will say unto me, and what I shall answer when I am reproved" (Habakkuk 2: 1).

It takes time to birth a vision. Ideas do not just drop from the skies. Spend some time to pray for the Lord to make clear his vision for your life. When an idea forms in your mind, spend some time praying and meditating upon it until it sinks into your heart. It may require separating yourself in prayer from things that distract you. Once the vision enters your heart, it starts to consume you. Until you spend time meditating on something, it would not take seed. Think about it and analyse it, and you will see it take shape. Do not discard that inner thought the Holy Spirit has given you. As you spend time in God's presence praying for a vision, he will drop an idea into your heart.

2. Write Your Vision and Document Your Ideas

"And the Lord answered me, and said, write the vision, and make it plain upon tables, that he may run that readeth it" (Habakkuk 2: 2).

Do not leave things to chance. You can easily forget ideas that have been birthed in your spirit as you wait on the Lord. Sometimes God plants an idea into your heart, and if it is not written somewhere, it disappears. There have been times when I have stopped my car whilst driving and pulled by the roadside to jot down an idea or an excerpt when I was writing this book. This is because by the time I get to my destination, that idea would probably have disappeared.

You cannot execute an idea (running with it) that has disappeared. Develop the habit of storing the vision in some form or in a way so that it is always at the forefront of your thoughts.

3. Patiently Work towards Its Accomplishment

"For the vision is yet for an appointed time, but at the end it shall speak, and not lie: though it tarry, wait for it; because it will surely come, it will not tarry" (Habakkuk 2: 3).

Understand that the vision itself is not the finished product. Most visions take years to come to fruition or fulfilment. God had a plan for each of these four men: Joseph, Moses, David, and Daniel. It took years for them to get to their destination or expected ends, and I see your vision being fulfilled in Jesus's name.

During a recent visit to Dubai, a gentleman drove my wife and me around the city. Whilst waiting at a lobby, I noted a picture of the ruler of the Emirates and made a comment that I admired his vision. The gentleman's response suggested how much the Emirates appreciated the Sheikh as a good leader and visionary. He was also keen to point out that the development I was seeing was only 20 per cent of the original vision and that 80 per cent was yet to be accomplished. Since the Sheikh birthed the vision, the vision still burns alive and is driving the strides that the Emirates have made in just a few years. I learnt that every accomplishment requires a visionary. To see all that development was testament to the fact that just about anybody, any group, and any race living in any part of the world can succeed if they have vision and the will to succeed.

A dream always starts as an insignificant thought and gradually takes form. It is just like a beautiful building. When you initially purchase your piece of land to build a house, you never have an idea what the final product will be. You may have an idea how it is going to be like from the original architectural drawings or plan but as the building progresses many changes happen that shapes the product.

So do not give up on yourself. You can accomplish much if you believe. Do not discard that burning desire, idea, or vision.

It is my prayer that God will grant you divine wisdom to birth visions. May you have supernatural foresight, and may your vision not be terminated or aborted in Jesus's name.

7

Value Time and Utilise Opportunities

> Again, I observed this on earth: the race is not always
> won by the swiftest, the battle is not always won by
> the strongest; prosperity does not always belong to
> those who are the wisest, wealth does not always
> belong to those who are the most discerning, nor
> does success always come to those with the most
> knowledge—for time and chance (or opportunity)
> may overcome them all.
>
> —Ecclesiastes 9: 11 (NLT)

Most of the time, the swiftest athlete wins a sprint and the strongest
boxer wins the fight. However, Solomon is right in that the race is not
always won by the swiftest. In a field of eight gifted 100m runners,
it is not always the most naturally gifted runner that wins the race.
There are always other factors, such as how fast you respond to the
starter gun, the type of running shoes you wear, the kind of track you
trained on, race strategy, and your mental conditioning. All these
factors make a difference as to who wins.

Again, if size and strength of arms was what wins a fight, then

Mike Tyson would have stood no chance against Trevor Berbick or Larry Holmes. Time and again he knocked out opponents much bigger and stronger than he was. He had an innate ability and a certain 'street streak' that perhaps others could not match. He also had ring-craft the others could not counter.

In the same vein, the fact that someone is deemed wise or discerning does not automatically confer prosperity and wealth on them if they ignore the wise use of time and opportunities. Similarly, success does not necessarily come to those with knowledge. There are many of us who have been adequately educated and acquired a lot of letters after our names but are not wealthy. In my country, Ghana, you can easily come across a university lecturer who is poor despite all the wealth of knowledge he or she possess. But in that same country, you will find someone who has never been to school yet is wealthy.

Solomon, I believe, was trying to say that in addition to being swift, strong, wise, discerning, and knowledgeable, you must learn to value time and utilise your chances (opportunities or resources) very well. If you ignore this time-honoured principle, then you can be as endowed as Africa is with all the riches in the world but will remain poor. In Ecclesiastes 10: 7, Solomon writes: "I have seen servants upon horses, and princes walking as servants upon the earth".

Time Is a Resource—Understanding Times and Seasons

Time is money, says the great adage. I have come to understand that our life is governed by time and every living creature's life is divided into seasons. An understanding that your life is made up of seasons will enable you to accomplish what needs to be accomplished at the right time in the right season.

My understanding of time being a great resource has been deepened by living in the developed world and by observing men and women who have achieved and continue to achieve great things. Just as any asset is managed well, so must time.

As I stated in previous chapters, many of us have dreams, visions, and aspirations, but have not been able to translate these into reality simply because we lack an understanding of how vital time and seasons are to the realisation of that vision.

"For everything there is a season, and a time for every matter (every purpose) under heaven" (Ecclesiastes 3: 1 ESV). This essentially means nothing happens by chance and that events must happen in chronological order if one must achieve his or her potential. This is by no means easy to achieve because there is no way we can predict the future or know what we are meant to be doing from one season to another. However, we can also deduce that life happens in seasons or phases. From birth, each of us goes through the following developmental stages: infancy to childhood to adolescence to adulthood. For each stage of our life are milestones that are expected to be achieved. At each stage, some changes are expected to happen. Each stage of development is needed for the next phase of your life to begin.

In primary school you are taught basic things so you can understand the more complicated things in secondary school, and in secondary school you build upon the foundations of primary education to prepare you for learning at a higher level where a lot of analytical thinking is required. So each season depends on the season before to help you progress. If you can understand this concept, then at every stage you will assess your life and strive to improve for a better tomorrow. Every day you wake up in the morning you are a day older and a day wiser—but also a day closer to your grave. That time lost can never be recovered. It is forward ever, backward never.

I want you to understand that time is a great resource. It is available to every person. Each of us has access to twenty-four hours in a day, seven days in a week, and 365 (or 366) days in a year. How you utilise this great resource can be the difference between mediocrity and greatness. How are prime ministers and presidents, CEOs and high-profile people able to manage time so efficiently to accomplish great things and yet many of us do not seem to have enough? Again, I realise it all comes down to the efficient use of time.

In a certain part of the world, time is of no essence. Time stands still whenever there are functions. Nothing is executed on time or planned with time. People can arrive at functions at any time and leave whenever. In that part of the world time is never seen as a resource, like many other resources that are wasted because there is no perception about it. Even when you take a person from that part of the world and place them in another part of the world where time governs everything, nothing changes. We can sit around and loiter for hours without taking stock of what we do in that time. We waste this precious resource all the time.

We are so hard pressed for time these days. There seems not to be enough to accomplish anything. Or is there? We appear under pressure and often hear people bemoaning how little time they have. Not enough to study, tidy the house, have a holiday, study for an exam, and other things? Is this really the case? Or maybe we have not learnt how to manage time efficiently.

Many times you hear people complaining about the lack of time to do this and that, but when you critically analyse what they do with their time you realise how much of it could have been purposefully used. We can sit and watch movies for hours or sports for that matter without getting bored. A good four to six hours are spent watching one game. Some people can spend a whole Sunday watching three football games back to back. However, it is so tedious for the same person to sit in church for two hours on Sunday listening to the Word of God and absorbing time-honoured wisdom which can transform their lives.

I believe that quality utilisation of time is important if we are to maximise our potential and break forth. I also sincerely believe that you can still accomplish your vision in so few years if you use time profitably. Just remember how long it has taken Dubai to move from what used to be called Old Dubai to what is now New Dubai.

The Key to Valuing Time

"Making the very most of your time (on earth, recognising and taking advantage of each opportunity and using it with wisdom and diligence), because the days are (filled with) evil. (Evil refers to the challenges we face)" (Ephesians 5: 16 AMP).

"So teach us to number our days that we may apply our hearts to wisdom" (Psalm 90: 12).

"And of the children of Issachar, which were men that had understanding of the times, to know what Israel ought to do" (1 Chronicles 12: 32).

Learn to value time. Learn to value each day—it is called numbering the days so that each day has a value, and each day of your week will be profitable. Every minute matters despite the challenges we face daily. Work when you must work, work diligently, and play when you must play. Both go hand in hand. Every precious day wasted cannot be recovered. Nobody is born with the wisdom to manage time wisely. It is an art you must consciously develop. Successful people have found a way to do so. Fortunately, we are blessed with many tools to help us manage our day: diaries, Microsoft Outlook, phones with reminders, and alarm clocks, among others. There are so many things to help us organise our day to make it fruitful. It does not mean living life like a robot, but it also does not mean living a carefree life with no sense of purpose.

Paul admonishes us to see that time waits for no man. Recognise that every valuable time wasted is an asset thrown away. The psalmist asks God to teach him how to utilise time and seasons wisely.

You can do so much in Thirty minutes

Did you realise that you can accomplish so much in just thirty minutes if you put your mind to it? You could listen to a whole preaching message. You can walk briskly for about two miles in twenty to thirty minutes to keep fit. You can read several chapters of a book. Recently I realised that if I put my mind to the task, I could easily write a chapter in thirty minutes. Isn't it amazing how much we can accomplish in that short amount of time?

Anytime I have sat on a commuter train from my local area to the city of London, a journey that takes an average of thirty minutes, I note some people striking deals on their laptops whilst others are idling or perhaps resting. In simple terms, you get paid for the time you spend doing something. A lawyer will charge you based on the hours of work they put in, and architects, plumbers, engineers, carpenters, or mechanics charge you for their hours. This means that for every minute of work done, you are either earning or gaining something. Therefore, the more of your time you can put into work, the more of a harvest you will generate. Conversely, the less time you put to fruitful use, the more you are likely to end up in poverty.

A few years ago I discovered that it took me roughly two to three hours to mow my front and back gardens. It was quite a chore that sometimes took longer, but the job was not nicely done. Then I got a gardener to do the same job whilst I did other work in those same two hours. I could earn roughly five times what I paid the gardener to do the job in that same time. In a way it was a win-win situation—getting a professional job done by utilising time efficiently and still making a tidy profit. This was accomplished by effective time management.

Years ago, the lock to my main front door at home was faulty. I called a locksmith to fix the problem. Within the space of five minutes he had completed the job. He handed me an invoice for a charge of £75.00. I questioned why I had to pay that amount for a job that lasted five minutes. His response was that the call-out charge per hour was £75 whether the job lasted five or sixty minutes. I paid with a very heavy and bitter heart. The only good thing was that I observed how he fixed the lock so the next time it malfunctioned, guess what I did.

I come from a cultural background where time stands still, where time appears not to be valued, and where life just passes by as if there is no tomorrow. Time is of no essence where I come from, and there is no hurry to accomplish anything. It is a culture where the preparation of a meal of palm soup and fufu can take an entire day, from the morning when your mum goes to the market until the evening when the meal is finally ready. In that same culture, when you invite someone to a function, he or she will usually turn up one to three hours late, and this is considered the norm. It appears we do not take account of time and have no sense of urgency. We have not learnt to value time and therefore cannot be bothered when it just passes by.

This situation is even worse now as people become more hedonistic and pleasure-seeking. We are encouraged to have more leisure time. Life has been made easier with scientific inventions, and we are encouraged to save the time and spend it having pleasure. Students can spend hours of valuable time on Facebook, Twitter, WhatsApp, and many other social media networks and yet complain about the college workload, which they cannot find time to complete. Have you worked out how much time you waste on unfruitful chit-chat, tête-à-tête, leisure, or watching useless TV programmes which have not enhanced your life in any way?

A young apprentice can watch television for hours rather than spending that time developing his or her skill. The value you place on something depends on how precious it is to you and determines what benefit you get out of it. Just as an expensive Rolex watch is of little value to a 5-year-old, so is time not of value to a man devoid of wisdom. Be wise, do not allow things to steal your time: too much leisure, too much pleasure, and too much sleep, and always engaging in useless conversation can steal your time and with it, the opportunity to excel. Galatians 6: 7 says, "Be ye not deceived, whatsoever a man sows doth shall he reap".

It takes great diligence to efficiently use time but then it is a key to success. If a young person can learn how to utilise the seasons of their life effectively, they will do well in life. This means study when you must (at a time when your parents or someone is paying the bills—the summer of your life) and work when you must.

As a young Christian, understand that your youthful days are the summer of your life. This is the period to lay the foundations for successful future living. If you waste this crucial period of your life, then the future will be filled with anxiety and difficulties unless the grace of God intervenes. You must understand and value your youthfulness. This is not the time to be chasing useless visions, chasing after money, indulging in fornication, and other useless vices that plague young people. It is time to love and work for the Lord and focus on developing yourself through education and apprenticeships.

Proverbs 10: 5 says, "He that gathereth in summer is a wise son: but he that sleepeth in harvest is a son that causeth shame". Use your time profitably. Be wise and discerning. May the Holy Spirit grant you the grace and wisdom to develop the art of efficient time management.

What Is Chance or Opportunity?

In his infinite wisdom, God has endowed every part of the earth with some godly pearls. Man, in his insatiable quest for success and greener pastures, sometimes leaves his natural habitat to sojourn to faraway lands for better and sunnier climes. But I have come to realise, rather belatedly, that you can virtually succeed anywhere if you can apply the principles of success. You see, principles are certain to work wherever they are applied. That is why a businessperson who succeeds in Africa could also succeed in Europe, even though the people, culture, and conditions are different. There are so many opportunities that come our way but either go unnoticed or we simply waste them. Sometimes we are not even aware that a set of circumstances represents an opportunity. We cannot see the multitude of opportunities that pass by us every hour. It takes perception to identify an opportunity, and that means carefully thinking about and focusing on the set of circumstances you are presented with. Even an adversity is an opportunity to progress, but many of us never see adversities as an opportunity.

If you can utilise the opportunities that come your way, then you could turn anything into a resource that can be used to your advantage. A stone can become a diamond, and people have even found usefulness for human excreta (faeces).

Many Great Accomplishments Have Been Borne of Small Opportunities

God blesses us with so many opportunities. The people we meet along life's journey constitute opportunities. This means that your father, mother, siblings, friends, teachers, supervisors, managers, pastors, and every person you directly encounter or have the chance to have contact with represents an opportunity to make it in life.

"Great moments are born from great opportunities"—Herb Brooks, hockey player and coach.

The job you are doing now or did in the past could be that opportunity to the breakthrough you are now looking for. That person God brought into your life may be the stepping stone to the realisation of that vision. Life is all about people.

The blessing comes from how you see things in relation to your vision. Perception is different from ordinary vision. We can all see objects if we are not blind, but how do we interpret what we see?

What you see is always what you get. How you perceive something, and how much value you place on someone or something will determine how much benefit you get out of it. Beauty lies in the eyes of the beholder.

Two people can see something, and one may see potential in it while the other may just see it as a waste of time. Many years ago, in Africa, people used to play with diamonds which they used as weapon for killing birds, but years later someone else from another continent saw the same stone and realised it was treasure.

Jesus taught on the principle of placing value on the little things we have. In Matthew 14: 20 (also Mark 6: 43 and John 6: 12), after feeding the five thousand, Jesus taught the disciples to gather the fragments so that none will be lost. Here, Jesus was trying to teach the disciples that one of the ways to live in abundance was to respect the small things that came our way. He was trying to point out to the disciples that they should not overlook little gains, small steps, the little things they took for granted because they are equally as important as the big things. He taught them to place value on things that appeared to be worthless. He also taught them about utilising resources to maximum benefits.

Many of us want sudden big breakthroughs, but they only come if we can value the small breakthroughs that come our way. Many of us do not respect those seemingly small opportunities. We lack insight, have no wisdom or discernment to understand that the journey takes time.

How do you treat that cleaning job you currently have or manage the little money you have? How did you treat the housing support a friend gave you or the pastors or spiritual fathers God brought your way, the husband God gave you, and even your parents?

Some were given opportunities to serve in church: leading a small group, playing a keyboard, drums, singing, ushering, cleaning, and even making tea for the pastor but saw it as menial chores. They had no clue that these opportunities were stepping stones to greater things. Some ignored that opportunity whilst others grabbed it with both hands. Look around you in church, and you probably may find a lot of people who are wasting time by not honouring the invitation to do something in church. After all, it was only when David humbly took food (corn, loaves, and cheese) to his brothers on the battlefield that he had the opportunity to fight Goliath. The rest is history. The next time an opportunity comes your way, recognise it.

Do you realise that not everyone has a British, EU, or American passport and therefore the opportunity to utilise the benefits of living in these economies?

Do you understand that if you live in a place like the United States or United Kingdom or any part of the western world, you have information at your fingertip to improve yourself? What do you do in your spare time, and how do you manage it? All this may seem trivial, like the fragments that were almost wasted by the disciples. If you put them all together, they make a basketful of blessings. If you can learn to identify every opportunity that comes your way, in no time you will fulfil your potential.

Each tiny snowflake easily melts into insignificance, but if you gather all the snowflakes and put them together, you get ice cubes, a snowman, or a glacier. You get prosperous not by winning the lottery (it is the easiest way to quickly get rich but does not happen every day) but by being wise with your pennies.

Many years ago, when I was a university student, I travelled overseas as a student to do holiday jobs. I made a few bucks but my prodigal attitude to money meant I spent it extravagantly on the university campus. At the time I did not have any financial wisdom or anyone to advise me. I was not even aware that the money I was earning could have bought plots of land. In those years I was a spendthrift. I remember walking into the bank one day to withdraw money. As I stood in the queue, a young boy, not more than 12, stood ahead of me in the queue. He was carrying his shoeshine box. Shoe shiners in Ghana clean and polish people's shoes for a living. This boy came to save twenty-seven cedis and ten pesewas (both currencies of Ghana) in his account. I had gone to the bank to withdraw money, far more than what this young boy came to deposit on that day. At the time I did not understand the significance of what this boy had done, storing his fragments, but years later as I learnt the lessons of prodigality, frugality, and managing wealth, it became clear how wasteful I had been.

Whilst this little boy valued the GHC 27.10 cedis, I treated the same amount as fragments. I was not even living in abundance, but because I did not know how to value pennies, I wasted my resources. I could have invested my fragments wisely, and who knows, with a little wisdom, I could be wealthy now.

During my days on the university campus, there was another gentleman who used to carry a small tray on his head to sell audio cassettes and other household goods to students. He would come around the various halls carrying his tray. I came to know him when I started first year. By the time I left campus seven years later, he owned two shops on campus and one large shop in the town. How did he do this? By valuing the small amount of money (fragments) he was generating through this small business.

I learnt then you do not always need millions of pounds or dollars or cedis to build a house. By the careful planning and wise utilisation of one's pennies, you can also build a house. Your ability to effectively manage your time, money, opportunities, and resources effectively will guarantee you a lifetime of success. If you need anything, it is wisdom and insight to identify what opportunities come your way and how to effectively use these.

Insignificant People and Enemies Can Also Represent Great Opportunities

Naaman (2 Kings 5) was a respected and esteemed commander with powerful political connections. He was also a successful person who commanded authority. But he was not complete. He had leprosy, then an incurable condition. You can actually imply that every one of us has a weakness or problem we do not seem to have an answer to but that answer or solution may always lie with someone else who usually may be close to us. None of us is perfect. You will always need to depend on someone for something.

The answer to Naaman's leprosy was in the hands of his wife's maid. In the grand scheme of things, a maid is not the most attractive source of cure for a great man. She may even be uneducated, less learned, and insignificant. Most of us see some of the blessing that come our way as 'little maids'—little and insignificant—but these insignificant jobs or opportunities are the open doors to the great blessings that lie ahead of us. Do you value the people around you?

Could it be that your business is not flourishing because you have not valued those around you? Is it possible that your relationship is not functioning because you are not placing any value on your spouse or partner? Or maybe you are failing in ministry because you do not treasure that little role you have been given at this point in your life. Naaman chose to follow the advice of this maid, though she was insignificant, and his leprosy was cured. If he had followed his pride, he would still have been incomplete. Many of us have still not fulfilled our real potential in ministry because we have not appreciated those God has placed over us. May we have eyes that see opportunities.

Can you learn something from your current boss, supervisor, manager, or even your employees? I want you to understand that the people around you are there for a reason, so begin to see them differently. Even if they are your enemies, they have been strategically placed there by the Lord. Begin to treat the people around you positively, and you will truly be blessed.

Learn to use your time wisely and maximise the opportunities that come your way. Be wise like the ant that works when it must work, taking advantage of the seasons to gather. Do not be like the grasshopper that has no wisdom to manage time and opportunities.

Opportunities Can Be Borne of Adversity and Trials

One thing that inspires me is how God has used trials, tribulations, and opportunities to bless his people as well bring glory to himself. Sometimes, when faced with a trial or challenge or adversity, many of us never see the hand of God in that situation. The loss of a job, loss of a loved one, a business that collapsed, or feelings of persecution could be opportunities to break forth. We are more likely to be affected in a negative way by the adversity than see it as an opportunity to be great. God works in mysterious ways. His ways are not our ways, and his thoughts are not our thoughts (Isaiah 55: 8–9). Sometimes it is his way. "The steps of a good man are ordered by the Lord" (Psalm 37: 23).

God has prepared a great future for you but the road to this great future may not necessarily come the easy way. It may be borne out of unusual circumstances. When one door of opportunity shuts, God usually directs you through his preferred door (orders your steps). When the apostles were persecuted in Jerusalem and dispersed, little did they know it was God's way of taking them out of their comfort to greatness.

Adversity forces you to look at other choices and pay close attention to options that had existed but which you were blind to.

God prepared a land flowing with milk and honey for the Israelites and instructed them move and take possession (Joshua 1: 1–4). However, the land was without its challenges including giants, Anakim, and hostile neighbours. They were expected to trust in God and face the adversity to enjoy the blessing. The destinies of Joseph, Moses, David, and Daniel were all associated with trials they had to face but led to great blessings. Therefore, if at present you are going through challenges, pray that God will open your eyes to see the opportunities within this adversity.

"Turn your obstacles into opportunities and your problems into possibilities"—Zimbabwean politician Roy Bennett.

As a young person with potential, you must learn to utilise the opportunities that come your way. You have youthfulness on your side, time, energy, good health, and some resources. The people that God brings your way—pastors, leaders, parents, supervisors, and others all represent opportunities. How you relate to them will affect your life. Everything is in your hands now, and around you may be opportunities from God to fulfil your dream.

"Poor is he who works with a negligent and idle hand, but the hand of the diligent makes him rich. He who gathers during summer and takes advantage of his opportunities is a son who acts wisely, but he who sleeps during harvest and ignores the moment of opportunity is a son who acts shamefully" (Proverbs 10: 4–5 AMP).

Try to apply the wisdom in the Word of God, and make changes to your current lifestyle, and by the grace of God, you will excel.

I pray that the Lord will grant you divine wisdom and prudence to manage your time and opportunities.

8

Make Investments in Yourself

Till I come, give attendance to reading, to exhortation, to doctrine. Neglect not the gift that is in thee, which is given thee by prophecy, with laying on of the hands of the presbytery. Meditate upon these things; give thyself wholly to them; that thy profiting may appear to all

—1 Timothy 4: 13–15

Why You Must Develop Yourself

Having a gift or talent is not enough. The talent is the raw material and must be developed. Talent on its own will not bring you success and must be developed.

There are many of us who are gifted in many ways, but during our development we stand still. We do not progress because we stop learning; we stop improving and stagnate. To remain at the very top you must constantly improve yourself. This is because as soon as you stand still you become stagnant and then fade away. The world we live in is very dynamic, and what is in vogue today becomes obsolete the next day. People are always seeking new adventures, thrills, excitement, and new ways of doing things. It is why you must never rest on your laurels and think you have arrived at the destination. The day you do so will be the beginning of your end. You must constantly seek knowledge, develop skill, and improve yourself. One of the reasons you must develop yourself is that you need more than just talent to survive at the top.

In 1 Timothy 4: 13–15, the apostle Paul makes it abundantly clear that when God gives you a talent or gift, there is work that must be done by you in developing it. You must not neglect your gift but must strive to develop it. You must be totally devoted to whatever you are doing, otherwise it will not be profitable to you or those for whom it is meant to be beneficial.

Invest in your gift by acquiring the necessary skill or knowledge, and practice wisdom that goes with your profession or talent. Investing in yourself and your gifts prepares you to take advantage of future opportunities that may come your way. There is nothing more painful than waiting for a breakthrough and being unprepared when it appeared. Preparation lays the foundation for future success.

The Key of Preparation Lays the Foundation for the Future

Each of us has opportunities for breakthroughs, but the question remains whether we will be prepared when those opportunities come our way. Your experiences, education, and apprenticeship prepares you for the opportunities that lie ahead. The importance of preparation is highlighted in this scripture: "If the foundations be destroyed, what can the righteous do?" (Psalm 11: 3) Without the foundation of preparation, you cannot build anything.

"If the axe is dull and he does not sharpen its edge, then he must exert more strength; but wisdom (to sharpen the axe) helps him succeed (with less effort)" (Ecclesiastes 10: 10 AMP). In simple terms, if you do not invest in yourself now, or do not prepare now, then you are bound for a life of struggles and failure in the future.

The Example of David

David honed his skills when tending sheep, and when the opportunity arose to play for King Saul, he was ready. He probably did not attend any music school or had private lessons playing the harp, but his attitude to learning and diligence to practice made him skilful. We are not told if he was trained to play, but for someone spending time with sheep all the time, he most likely taught himself. He did not know that as he kept practising, he was honing a skill that took him to the palace. He did not neglect the gifts God gave him: the ability to write songs, sing psalms, and play music.

David probably did not know that looking after sheep and being interested in their welfare was preparing him to lead people. Fighting with lions and bears equipped him with the courage to tackle much bigger challenges in the form of Goliath. It can be said that his preparatory ground was in that obscure desert or wilderness where no one was watching. He kept doing the same thing until his encounter with Goliath. He was not even aware that the errand he was sent on was to lead to his breakthrough. Never despise your small beginnings.

It is amazing that God was impressed by David's qualities of being dedicated to sheep and saw that as a mark of someone who was faithful with what seemed insignificant to others. "He chose David also his servant and took him from the sheepfolds: from following ewes great with young he brought him to feed Jacob his people, and Israel his inheritance. So, he fed them from the integrity of his heart; and guided them by the skilfulness of his hands" (Psalm 78: 70–72).

The story of David is mirrored by Joseph whose service in the house of Potiphar and in prison prepared him for the higher office of prime minister. By being a steward in a home and in prison, he was prepared to take care of the far greater resources of a nation after micromanaging on a small scale.

"If I had eight hours to chop down a tree, I'd spend six sharpening my axe"—Abraham Lincoln

Lincoln was saying that it is equally important to spend time preparing yourself for an opportunity so that when it arrives you can grab it with both hands. Investing in yourself involves investing in knowledge and skill. It also means continually staying current with the times and being abreast with current thinking and way of doing things.

Be Knowledgeable in Your Area of Skill and Discipline

"My people are destroyed for lack of knowledge" (Hosea 4: 6). Knowledge is power. Knowledge is illuminating and empowers people (Ecclesiastes 7: 12). People are easily deceived and indoctrinated and mentally enslaved when do not seek or have knowledge (Luke 11: 52). The three wise men in the Bible were considered wise because they had wisdom, and acquisition of the right knowledge helps an individual break out of poverty and non-achievement.

In 2 Timothy 2: 15, Paul admonished Timothy, a pastor, to strive and become an excellent pastor. Paul highlights one of the benefits of improving oneself in your area of skill—preventing shame, as you could be found out at the very top when the going gets tough. Paul was also pointing out to Timothy that if he did not spend time and effort investing in the word of God, he was more likely to become a 'cowboy preacher', someone who lacks knowledge and skill at handling the word of God and is likely to be a liar or thief, manipulating the truth of the word of God and deceiving the congregation.

It is for the same reason we have 'cowboy' electricians, plumbers, builders, and surgeons. It is why many professionals join approved bodies so that their knowledge and skill can be certified. Without investing in knowledge and skill in your area of discipline, you will eventually be found out.

Can you imagine doctors who do not update their knowledge and skill? They will still be practicing medicine from the dark ages and therefore killing people mercilessly.

The prophet Daniel was studious and gained understanding not just by the holy spirit but also through studying books. (Daniel 9: 2).

Daniel was a prophet but in addition to the gift of interpreting dreams and visions, he also developed that skill and knowledge by gaining further knowledge through reading.

Paul also studied so much from books and he had notes and excerpts (parchments) (2 Timothy 4: 13). Investing in yourself to enhance your talent takes time and costs money, but it is necessary.

Develop Your Mind—It Is Where the Battle Is Won or Lost

The mind is the part of the brain responsible for reasoning and for one's thoughts and feelings. It is the seat of thinking and crucial for imagination, perception, judgement, and emotions.

Proverbs 23: 7 says, "For as he thinketh in his heart, so is he". The way your mind functions can be the difference between succeeding and failing. How your mind works is reflected in your personality, actions, and attitude. Your way of thinking depends on several external factors: birth place, where you grew up, the community you grew up in, schools you attended, the kind of parents and family you had, as well as your personal experiences. What you have been exposed to as you grew up and the experiences you have had on life's journey all shape your thinking. It is important to develop the mind so you can cultivate a winning mentality.

Develop the Mind with Knowledge

"And do not be conformed to this world [any longer with its superficial values and customs], but be ye transformed and progressively changed [as you mature spiritually) by the renewing of your mind [focusing on godly values and ethical attitudes], so that you may prove [for yourselves] what the will of God is, that which is good and acceptable and perfect [in his plan and purpose for you]" (Romans 12: 2 AMP).

The right information from the right source will always transform your thinking and change your personality for the better. If you can alter the way you think, and then you can change the direction of your life. Your destiny changes if you transform how you think about yourself and your old way of doing things.

Progress is all about the mind—success and failure, joy or sorrow, depression or happiness. There is some pathology that can affect a person's way of thinking, but by and large your way of thinking may make the difference between being an achiever and being a failure.

The centre point of control is the mind. Once you can control it, direct it, and renew it, then you can begin to change things. Elephants, lions, and gorillas are all bigger and stronger than man, but man controls every other living creature by exercising his superior mind.

Amongst people, those who rule have managed to exercise this dominion by and large by using their mind to a certain degree to gain that advantage. Most rich people have become richer by exercising the power of thinking, and some poor people have become poorer because they have refused to think.

Africa has more resources than the rest of the world, comparatively more in terms of land size. However, amid the abundant resources, they are counted amongst the poorest. Why? Due to the mindset of its leaders and to a great extent its people.

"But be ye transformed by the renewing of your mind" (Romans 12: 2). Transformation comes when the mind is renewed with new information. A person can change the way he or she thinks from being a failure to becoming successful just by acquiring the right information or knowledge.

It should not come as a surprise to see a previously dangerous armed robber transform and become as docile as a dove when exposed to the word of God for a long time. In the same way, an intelligent, skilful, gentle person can be indoctrinated and transformed to become a hardened terrorist or killing machine.

You must be flexible and willing to change your way of thinking. Matthew 9: 17 says, "Neither do men put new wine into old bottles: else the bottles break, and the wine runneth out, and the bottles perish: but they put new wine into new bottles, and both are preserved".

Jesus was talking about the pharisees who were not amenable and adaptable to his teaching. They were entrenched in their beliefs and resisted any new way of thinking with all their might. Jesus was demonstrating that it is quite difficult to change the mindset of someone who is entrenched in their way of thinking. This means that to turn someone's life around they must renew their thinking. Transformation only happens through renewing of the mind with new knowledge.

To be able to embrace change you, must change how you think. An ex-convict keeps re-offending despite many sessions of CBT and rehabilitation because his or her way of thinking has not changed. If you can change the mindset, you change the person.

Old wineskins are rigid, fixed, and cannot expand. For it to hold new wine, it must be softened and adapted for this purpose. If this does not happen, the wineskin will burst, the content wasted. Fresh wine has been fermented and will explode if placed in these old wineskins. Therefore, new wine must be put in new wineskins.

In much the same way, if you want to change the direction of your life—for example from one of addiction, alcoholism, gambling, poverty, abuse, or low self-esteem—you must change the way you think. If you renew the mind, you can change the direction of your life. If a person is not willing to change and is not flexible to embrace a new way of thinking, he or she could even end up being destroyed by the change.

"Progress is impossible without change, and those who cannot change their minds cannot change anything"—George Bernard Shaw.

God does not put fresh ideas into fossilized minds. Old habits and attitudes must change. Old ways of thinking and doing things must change. Old habits must give way to new habits. Do this and the opportunities open up for you. The mind is renewed through the acquisition of new information or knowledge. The knowledge that is available to you can also shape your life. It shapes your destiny.

I was surrounded by books when I was growing up. I grew up in a working-class background where our only chance of doing well was to study. The desire to become a doctor was ignited in me when I visited an uncle in Accra, Ghana, during a school holiday. I was a young, fresh-faced secondary school student. He is a medical doctor and has a library at home full of medical books. One day I wandered into his library and saw many books that described the human body. I got excited and immersed myself in those books. When I left for my village, I had developed the desire to become a doctor. My future career had suddenly been birthed, or framed, by those books and by what I had seen and read. The exposure to that knowledge shaped the direction of my life. It reinforces the fact that what we see, hear, and experience shapes our thinking and the direction of our lives. Knowledge is power.

Knowledge that can change your life is always costly. They are like pearls of wisdom. "Counsel in the heart of man is like deep water; but a man of understanding will draw it out" (Proverbs 20: 5). You do not just stumble upon wisdom. Anyone who wants to succeed in his or her field will do whatever it takes to acquire the knowledge and skill to do well in that area. There is always a price to pay for the right kind of knowledge.

When I was in sixth form, I did not have the resources to go for extra or private tutorials or special vacation classes. They were financially beyond my reach. I had several classmates who came from wealthy backgrounds and had the opportunity to get extra tutorials from some of the best teachers in the country.

However, my lack of financial resources was not to be a limitation. I made up with sheer hard work as some of my friends will testify. In those days, photocopiers had not been invented. There were no mobile phones to take pictures of notes. We had no access to e-mails, scanners, and computers. When my friends returned to school after vacation, I would go round, collect their notes from those vacation classes, and manually copy them into my own notebook. It was hard work, spending nights copying not just notes but past questions. I also spent time painstakingly going through questions and answering them using a marking scheme I copied from someone. I remember very clearly walking about twelve miles (round trip) to see someone in a neighbouring secondary school to collect the marking scheme because I had no money for transport. The sacrifices I made paid off as I passed my GCE A levels quite well.

This is just to buttress the point that you must pay the price to acquire the necessary knowledge and skill you need. There is no other way. The Bible describes wisdom as pearls and rubies, and these are costly to acquire. So be prepared to spend money, time, and effort on books, CDs, DVDs, courses, and other resources to improve yourself. Every investment you make in yourself spiritually and secularly will bear fruit.

Knowledge and skill are not only acquired through books but through association. Proverbs 13: 20 states: 'He who walks (as a companion) with wise men will be wise. But the companions of (conceited, dull-witted) fools (are fools themselves and) will experience harm" (AMP).

By associating with wise people, the knowledge, wisdom, and skillset you need to do well in life could be passed to you either directly or indirectly. When you associate with people who have more experience, knowledge, and skills in your area of work, you become better.

While training for his coaching badges in his mid-20s, Manchester United coach Sir Alex Ferguson stated: "I made sure that I got my coaching badges and to listen and observe how well-established coaches went about their jobs". Are we then surprised that he became one of the best managers in the world? He had an attitude to learn from the best.

I have been pastored by one of the best in ministry, Bishop Dag Heward-Mills, and I continue to learn from other great ministers within our church denomination. That association has made me a better person and minister and changed my destiny.

You may also have pastors or great people that are present in your life, but until you understand the purpose of their presence in your life, you will miss a great opportunity to break forth.

Assess Your Progress, and Take Stock of Your Life

"Be diligent to know the condition of your flocks and pay attention to your herds. For riches are not forever, nor does a crown endure to all generations" Proverbs 27: 23–24 AMP).

The Jamieson, Fausset, and Brown commentary on the bible explains that "flocks constituted the staple of wealth. It is only by care and diligence that the most solid possessions can be perpetuated".

Your flock and herds refer to your wealth, possessions, profession, skill or whatever you do for a living. In the days of Proverbs 27: 23, a man's wealth was usually judged by the size of their flock if they were farmers, and the state of the flock determined how wealthy one could become. Imagine that your flock were sick, diseased, and unproductive. It would lead to poverty.

In much the same way as a farmer assesses the quality of his crops after the harvest, must you assess your development at different points of your life. This will ensure that you move forwards and not backwards and have longer-lasting success in whatever you do. It also means that if you do not diligently assess your progress at any stage and take steps to improve your present state, you will slowly degenerate.

Plug the gaps in your knowledge, skills, and understanding every step of the way because as you climb higher, you need new information, skills, and wisdom to survive. When a plant stops growing, it starts to wither. In the same way, if you stop making investments in your development, your value will slowly depreciate.

I pray that you will understand the importance of investing in yourself as a way of breaking out and breaking forth. May the Lord enable you to do so in Jesus's name.

9

Have Control over Your Environment

And delivered just Lot, vexed with the filthy conversation of the wicked: for that righteous man dwelling among them, in seeing and hearing, vexed hid righteous soul from day to day with their unlawful deeds.

—2 Peter 2: 7–8

The Advanced English Dictionary defines *environment* as, "The area in which something exists or lives and the totality of surrounding conditions".

Whenever I hear people debating issues around nature versus nurture, I find it intriguing how many of us limit the effect the environment has on our ability to succeed.

I realise the environment that children grow in makes a huge impact on their future outcomes. This is because development is influenced by what you see, hear, and experience.

The potential (genetic ability, gifts or nature) in a seed is influenced a great deal by external factors. For example, if a seed is planted in an ideal soil (environment) and receives adequate sunshine, rain, and less competition (negative factors) it is likely to give maximum yield. In much the same way if you are gifted, then in the right environment you will do well. Therefore, you must endeavour to control your environment to make it suitable for yourself so that you can break out and succeed.

Every seed has potential, but there are factors that affect the seed which will determine whether it thrives or dies when placed in the soil. Seeds require the right environment to flourish, such as soil, water, adequate light, and nutrients, and it must be free from weeds.

A few years ago, I bought an indoor plant during the winter season. I neither read about this plant nor the conditions to care for it. I simply saw a nice indoor plant which I felt could be a nice addition to my indoor decor. In my ignorance, I thought every plant required the same basic needs of adequate sunlight, water, and soil nutrients for thriving. Some days later I took this potted plant and left it in the back garden because the day appeared sunny. I completely forgot about and left it out overnight. The next morning there was frost all over the leaves, but I assumed it would just thaw and the leaves will recover. The plant died within a few days. I took it back to the shop, complaining that the plant was of low quality and had died within a few weeks of purchase. After listening to my story, I was nicely advised that it was my poor care that killed the potted plant. I did not create the conditions conducive for it to survive. It was meant to be an indoor plant. I learnt lessons that every seed or plant required the right environment to thrive.

In much the same way your talent will be honed if the environment you find yourself in is right. However, you must also understand that you may have the power to modify your environment. The environment you need in order to thrive is greatly affected by what you see, the words you hear, and the company you keep.

You have the power to control and modify your environment by managing the following:

- The things you see or watch;
- The words you hear and listen to; and
- The company you keep (people you surround yourself with).

The things you see and hear can greatly affect your destiny. Words are powerful. Words can either make or break you. Anything you see or hear can affect you positively or negatively. Never underestimate the effects of words or the voices you hear or what you allow yourself to watch. We are all a sum of what we have experienced in our lives by the words we hear, the things we see, and the people with whom we associate.

The Story of Lot

In 2 Peter 2: 7–8, it says, "And delivered just Lot, vexed with the conversation of the wicked: for that righteous man dwelling among them, in seeing and hearing, vexed his righteous soul from day to day with their unlawful deeds".

Lot was a righteous man who initially dwelled in the plain of Jordan and pitched his tent toward Sodom (Genesis 13: 11–12). He was originally not living amongst the inhabitants of Sodom and Gomorrah. How he found himself later living in the city no one knows. Living amongst these people impacted greatly on his destiny. What he saw and heard daily, amongst the wrong company, had a great effect on the course of his life. The wrong choice of environment and company can seriously wreck your future.

Control What You Watch or See

It is true we may find it difficult to control a lot of the things we see these days but to a large extent, you can also monitor what you see, hear, or read. Much of what we read impacts us positively or negatively by affecting the way we think. The movies you watch and books you read speak to you directly or indirectly. You must understand that not everything is edifying to see or watch.

You may not be able to control what you see, but you can control what you watch. You cannot do anything about the endless advertising you have seen all through your life. You can allow it to just pass by, or you can focus on it and allow the message to influence your thought processes. Advertising, for example, is meant to appeal to your senses, change your perception about something, and influence your behaviour. But you have absolute control over what you choose to believe.

Control What You Hear, and Maintain an Environment of Positivity

It is difficult to control what we hear as the voices are external. Nevertheless, you can make a conscious effort not to allow certain things you hear influence you negatively.

Everything you hear has an impact on you either directly or indirectly, as scriptures makes clear: "There are, it may be, so many kinds of voices in the world, and none of them is without signification" (1 Corinthians 14: 10). Everything you hear has significance. Words are powerful and have an impact on your mind—and therefore on your well-being. Every word you hear must be deemed important to you. You must able to sift through and discard anything that can negatively impact on your life. Because if you do not, then your progress can be stifled.

"We understand that the worlds were framed by the word of God" (Hebrews 11: 3). If the worlds were created just by words being spoken, then understand that every word you have heard or spoken over your life will either make you or break you. You must make a conscious effort not to be around certain (negative) people or be in a certain kind of environment that will stifle your development.

We can either be inspired or discouraged by what we hear, because words can change the direction of your life. Ephesians 4: 29 says, "Do not let unwholesome (foul, profane, worthless, vulgar) words ever come out of your mouth, but only such speech as is good for building up others, according to the need and the occasion, so that it will be a blessing to those who hear (you speak)" (AMP).

Apostle Paul was clear that words spoken have the ability either to minister grace (enabling ability) or minister discouragement. If someone persistently spoke negative words about your potential, you could easily internalise this negative perception about yourself, and this can be soul destroying. The Bible makes it clear that death and life lie in the power of the tongue (Proverbs 18: 21). Through words, you can be encouraged to flourish, but your potential can also be destroyed.

Avoid Negative People

The words of the ten spies discouraged an entire nation, but the words of two inspired them. No wonder God said that Joshua had an excellent Spirit—Joshua and Caleb thought positively and this impacted their exploits (Numbers 13: 26–33, 14: 1).

Words have framed many a black man that "the black man is cursed". As a result, many of my kinsmen have internalised this, and rather than look for practical solutions to problems, we spent hours looking for spiritual deliverance. Many African men and women with great potential and an entrepreneurial spirit have been led to believe in some of these lies and superstitious beliefs. These able-bodied men and women could channel their skills and knowledge to achieve more rather than seek deliverance.

Wars have been won by the inspirational words of a leader or by the defeatist attitude of another leader. Great things have either been accomplished or destroyed because of derisory words (Nehemiah 2: 19).

David was a bold man—his words of faith enabled him to defeat Goliath. Saul and the other soldiers were dismayed by the words of Goliath (1 Samuel 17: 11). For forty days and nights, Goliath repeatedly said the same thing (17: 16, 23) until David's arrival.

David was not intimidated by Goliath's intimidating words (17:

26, 32, 34–37). When you contrast his words with the words of Saul (17: 33), who was then leading the army, is it any wonder that Israel dwelt on the plains for forty days without victory until the arrival of David?

David's brothers were discouragers. Eliab tried to pour scorn on David's ability as a warrior (17: 28). He made references to his background as a way of discouraging him. Eliab made an error of judgement; you cannot tell how great someone is going to be in future because of their present circumstances. David ignored him (17: 30), otherwise Eliab would have destroyed his breakthrough and denied Israel victory by his careless words. You must also learn to avoid people who try to devalue your worth and associate with people who are more likely to encourage you.

Discouragers are more likely to pour scorn on your ability or gifts. They are more likely to use words that discourage the little effort you make. You meet such people all through your life as spouses, managers, friends, family members, or bosses.

That is why sometimes nothing is achieved in an institution until an inspirational and bold leader appears on the scene, and the same group of underachieving people will suddenly begin to exceed expectations. Words are important, so your environment must be framed with the right words. When you hear appropriate words that reprove, that refresh your spirit, you are likely to do well. Words that are kind, when spoken at the right time (fitly spoken) will always lead to building you up.

Proverbs 25: 11 states, "Like apples of gold in settings of silver is a word spoken at the right time" (AMP). Hearing the right words at the right time for the right reasons will enable you to break forth in the right season. It is important you try and avoid, if you can, people who speak negative words, or situations that pollute your environment with negativity.

Watch the Company You Keep

"Be not deceived: evil communications corrupts good manners" (1 Corinthians 15: 33). People are social beings, and nobody can survive in isolation. We all need people around us, and most times we like to be accepted and appreciated by others. This means that most of us crave the company of others so we can be happy. You celebrate your success with people, and you share your sorrow with fellow humans and not inanimate objects. It is said that, "Joy shared is double joy and sorrow shared is sorrow halved". It is important to understand that if you need to develop potential, you must learn to keep the right company.

It is important to build a network of good friends who can give you genuine advice, not boot lickers and parasites who are only interested in what you can offer them. Good and reliable friends and associates will give you wise counsel, guidance, and direction when required. The Bible makes it clear: "Where no counsel is, the people fall: but in the multitude of counsel there is safety" (Proverbs 11:14)

The right friends and associates will help you make good decisions.

Surround Yourself with Like-Minded People

"Iron sharpeneth iron; so a man sharpeneth the countenance of his friend" (Proverbs 27: 17). You need to surround yourself with the right people if you want to break out and break forth. The wrong company can stifle your development just as the right company can push you on. The commonest example we use is that if you take a burning coal out of a fire full of burning coals, the fire in the isolated coal slowly dies off. This means that you need to be around progressive people to be progressive yourself.

"He that walketh with wise men shall be wise: but a companion of fools shall be destroyed" (Proverbs 13: 20). If you are surrounded by people who do not encourage you, then it is better to discard this company and acquaint yourself with the right group. You need to learn from successful people if you want to be successful.

Networking is so vital because as you reach higher, you need to surround yourself with important people. If you want to break forth, try to find company with the right people.

Create Support Systems

"And the Lord God said, It is not good that the man should be alone; I will make him an help meet for him" (Genesis 2: 18). Human beings are created to be social and depend on one another. Human beings are created to be interdependent. Nobody succeeds in isolation. No human being is an island. Naturally, we seek companionship. The human population has accomplished much by interacting and sharing with one another. Isolation can lead to social disaster.

No one is perfect. As we go through life, we can make mistakes. It usually takes an observer to point out our mistakes to us.

In times of stress, difficulty, and affliction you need company, a shoulder to lean on, someone who can not only rebuke or criticise constructively but can point the way forward. They must show empathy and genuine concern. This usually depends on trust within that relationship.

Who do you talk to in times of crisis? Who speaks into your life in your moments of difficulty? The counsel you get in difficult moments can either make or break you.

Presidents and prime ministers have advisors and counsellors. Why? So they will not make costly mistakes. "Two are better than one; because they have a good reward for their labour. For it they fall, the one will lift up his fellow: but woe to him that is alone when he falleth; for he hath not another to help him up" (Ecclesiastes 4: 9–10).

This means you always need to network with someone or a group of people because you will always face a crisis at some point. Everybody will need a shoulder to lean on. Make every effort to develop faithful and trustworthy friends who will be there to support you in times of difficulty.

I pray that God will grant you the insight and wisdom to choose the right friends.

Constantly Expose Yourself to New Environments

Networking increases your exposure. There are benefits of exposing yourself to new things. Broaden your horizons. When your vision is limited by a lack of knowledge, it does not grow. Expose yourself to new ways of doing things, new knowledge; travel to new places, discover new cultures, and embrace change, for life itself is made up of seasons. Things change all the time. New experiences make you better, enrich your life, and enhance your perception. They help you make better judgments and decisions. Have a flexible mindset, not a fixed mentality.

Anyone who is rigid and averse to change gets left behind or falls behind. It could lead to your vision remaining unfulfilled. You do not know it all. No one is a walking encyclopaedia. You can always learn something new from somebody; even a child can teach you something. So be open-minded and you will go far in life.

What you watch, read, and listen to may potentially be taking your life in the wrong direction. Make sure you control your environment. Make sure you associate with the right people, and be willing to change your mindset to make progress.

What we see and hear and our associations affect our destinies so much that God had to relocate Abraham, Joseph, and Moses so he could fulfil his long-term plan for their lives. God changed their environments because they were destined to become great leaders and needed to see the right things, hear the right things, have the right experiences, and be shaped by the right company.

It is my prayer that the Lord will grant you the strength and wisdom to make the required changes to your environment.

10

Find a Good Mentor

Every purpose is established by counsel: and with good advice make war.

—Proverbs 20: 18

Why Do We Need Mentors to Succeed?

Talent is like a seed. It needs the right environment to thrive. Without guidance and nurturing, talent may not blossom, and the gifted person may never achieve true potential.

Many of the best talents or potentially gifted young people can be the most difficult to nurture. This highlights the importance of having a mentor in your life if you desire to fulfil your true potential.

Who or what is a mentor? Let us look at a few definitions:

- "a person who gives a younger or less experienced person help and advice over a period of time, especially at work or school" (dictionary.cambridge.org)

- "a mentor is a more experienced individual willing to share knowledge with someone less experienced in a relationship of mutual trust" (www.coachingnetwork.org.uk);

From the above definitions we can glean many important key principles:

- the person doing the learning is 'young' (not necessarily due to age) and inexperienced in that field of discipline;
- the mentor is more experienced, more knowledgeable, and has the skill to teach, guide, counsel, and give you advice;
- through mentoring you receive help, advice, and guidance; and in addition, wisdom, knowledge, and experience, relevant to your development, is imparted to you.

You must understand from the definitions above that mentoring involves a trusted relationship; it is a process that takes time and involves a lot of communication between the mentor and mentee.

In the absence of the right mentoring, you may not receive the right counsel, advice, guidance, or the relevant knowledge, skills, and wisdom for your development. As a person with potential, if you do not get mentored at the right time, it may take you many years to fulfil your potential. The truth is that without someone offering you guidance, the only lessons you learn are mainly from the mistakes you make, which could be catastrophic. You can avoid many mistakes and pitfalls and shorten the time it takes to reach the top.

I realise that because the mentoring process takes a long time, the mentee needs to be humble and submissive so that the mentor can impart the required lessons.

Whilst mentoring is usually done face to face, you can adopt a mentor and learn from him or her through books, podcasts, and other audio-visual aids if you cannot have direct access to the mentor. Whether you are in ministry, sports, entertainment, or any other area of life including marriage, you need guidance to succeed.

A master has experience and can imagine the future. The mentee is a novice and needs guidance. His presence around the apprentice ensures that fewer mistakes are made. If on your own, your journey to success could take many years, but in the presence of a mentor it may less time. Experience sharpens your insight and enhances your perception.

I believe that most people who have succeeded usually get good guidance and counselling from others.

Mentoring Involves Guidance and Counselling

It is important to understand that the underlying principle of all forms of mentoring is counselling. The Bible highlights the key importance of counselling for success. Even kings, CEOs, and presidents surround themselves with counsellors.

"Where no counsel is, the people fall: but in the multitude of counsellors there is safety" (Proverbs 11: 14).

"Every purpose is established by counsel: and with good advice make war" (Proverbs 20: 18).

The scriptures highlight the following truths: counselling will keep you safe and preserve your life; you need good counsel before embarking in any meaningful venture; and any vision or project is manifested through good counsel.

Let us look at a few biblical examples of how good guidance and counselling resulted in successful outcomes.

Joseph Gives Guidance to His Family

Joseph had lived in Egypt for a considerable time and knew the country and its culture. As the prime minister, he also knew the best parts of the land to dwell on and thrive in. He understood what was unacceptable to the Egyptians and especially the thought processes of Pharaoh. When his father and family came to Egypt, he gave them sound advice regarding what to say to Pharaoh (Genesis 46: 33–34).

They heeded this advice (47: 3) and ended up dwelling in Goshen (47: 6).

Moses Receives Mentorship from Jethro

"Wisdom belongs to the aged, and understanding to the old" (Job 12: 12 NLT). Moses was leading the nation of Israel (numbering more than 144,000) out of Egypt to the promised land. His father-in-law, Jethro, was the priest of Midian pastoring a smaller flock. However, Jethro was older, wiser, and more experienced at man management compared to Moses. Despite the apparent stature of Moses, he still needed guidance and counselling from a more experienced minister who had been in the ministry much longer. Jethro observed how Moses judged the people (Exodus 18: 13–16) and then showed Moses what to do (18: 17–23). His advice was simple—he told him his methods would cause burnout in his ministry—and taught him how to share the burden. Moses listened to the counsel, which saved him from burnout and unusual stress that could have curtailed his mandate.

Esther Was Nurtured by Mordecai and Hegai

Esther was a young, uneducated, orphaned slave. Her humility and ability to heed counsel from both Mordecai and Hegai, the king's chamberlain, catapulted her from obscurity to becoming queen (Esther 2: 10–15). Mordecai had counselled her not to reveal her identity to anyone at the beginning, and this saved not just her life but that of the entire Jewish people. It is interesting to find in Esther 2: 13–15 that when the maidens were ready to be ushered into the presence of the king, they are given whatever they desired to go out. In verse 15 it says that when it was Esther's turn, she required nothing but what Hegai had recommended. Hegai knew the taste of the king more than even Mordecai. It made sense to trust his judgement. It takes wisdom to humble yourself under a mentor or great person. They know more, have seen more, experienced more, and have more to give you than you can give them. Be humble and you will be promoted.

Ruth Is Nurtured by Naomi

Ruth lived with Naomi, who was better skilled at predicting the moods of men and what it took to get the attention of a man. Her counsel to Ruth (Ruth 3: 3–5) helped her make a good catch in Boaz.

David's Future Heritage Is Saved by Abigail

David was young, brave, and prudent. But like every young man, he was not exempt from the odd rash decision resulting from adrenaline flow. He was on his way to kill Nabal and his men but was counselled by Abigail (1 Samuel 25: 24–31) to allow the Lord to fight his battles for him and ensure his future kingship was not tainted. David heeded this wise counsel, otherwise it may have come back to haunt him. Remember that in almost all previous battles he had inquired of the Lord. This would have been a battle he would have fought by following his emotions.

In all the cases above, good guidance and counselling led to divine purposes being established, and I believe that if you also allow yourself to be mentored, every purpose in your life will be established.

The Place of Yielding

It is not easy to stay with a mentor for many years. Just as any relationship can grow stale, so can the mentor-mentee relationship. There have been so many occasions when many gifted athletes or child prodigies have changed managers or coaches or trainers whom they felt were not good enough to take them forward. Most times it was because the relationship became fractious. You must learn to yield or submit to be able to learn and develop.

The key to being mentored successfully lies in humility and in having a childlike attitude to learning (Matthew 18: 2–3). A child looks gullible, has a believing attitude, and usually places his or her trust in the parent or guardian. That dependability enables the parent then to impart, cater to, and care for that child. Each one of us would have to be led by someone at some point in our lives. During that relationship, things may not be rosy, but don't develop the habit of always checking out when the going gets tough.

"If the temper of the ruler rises against you, do not leave your post (showing resistance), because composure and calmness prevent great offences" (Ecclesiastes 10: 4 AMP).

When you are gifted, pride and arrogance can make you feel powerful and good. You may think you know it all. When you have the wrong attitude to learning and being mentored, you may be gifted but may never fulfil your potential.

Cast your eyes around. I am sure you have either seen, heard, or read about famous celebrities or athletes who never went far in their careers because they had a bad attitude. Understand that good counselling and guidance play a major role in helping you break out and break forth.

It is my prayer that the Holy Spirit will lead you to the right people that God positioned along your pathway of life. May your steps be ordered by the Lord in Jesus mighty name.

11

Develop a Winning Mentality

For as he thinketh in his heart so is he.

—Proverbs 23: 7

The Mind Is the Battlefield and the Seat of Decision Making

Proverbs 23: 7 says, "For as he thinketh in his heart so is he". The mind is the part of the brain responsible for reasoning, thoughts, and feelings. It is the seat of thinking and crucial for imagination, perception, judgement, and emotions. The mind is the part of people that enables them to feel, think, reason, and makes judgments. It is also associated with perception, thoughts, and memory.

The way your mind functions can be the difference between succeeding and failing. How your mind works is reflected in your personality, your actions, and your attitude. Your way of thinking depends on several external factors: birth place, where you grew up, the community you grew up in, schools you attended, the kind of parents and family you had as well as your personal experiences in life.

What you have been exposed to as you grew up and the experiences you have had on life's journey (seen, heard, and felt) all shape your thinking. It is important to develop the mind so you can cultivate a winning mentality.

A person's mentality and ability to reason, process information, and manage his or her emotions influences the decisions made and actions taken. The mind is a particularly important part of a person. The ability to harness the powers of the mind to process information, reason, and make sound decisions has enabled man to have dominion over every other creature.

The mind is not the same as the brain. The brain is the physical organ in the skull that one can see, but you cannot physically see the mind.

In my short career as a general medical practitioner, I have had consultations with thousands of patients and leant some crucial lessons about how our mind functions.

One of my crucial observations has been that victory, as well as defeat, is a function of the mind. How a person's mind functions can affect progress in a positive or negative way. Your natural responses to events are generally a function of your mind. How you react to events is influenced greatly by how your mind processes information. You draw on whatever information is in your mind to make crucial decisions. This means that your successes and failures are possibly linked to decision making, which is a crucial function of the mind.

Many conditions can affect the mind, making it difficult for the individual to harness this important aspect of being. Conditions such as mental illness (Mark 5: 15), fear (Leviticus 26: 6), and doubt (Matthew 13: 31) affect the mind and the ability to process information.

Victory and defeat always begin in the mind even before the battle begins. How we perceive threats largely depends on how your mind works. The functioning of your mind depends on so many factors— temperament, knowledge gained, skillset, experiences, and the general personality of the person. Some people are naturally strong-willed and hold no fear irrespective of the anticipated threat whilst others naturally become anxious and panicky about the threat of danger.

The twelve spies sent by Moses to the Promised Land saw the same situation, but their attitude and responses to the situation were different.

The Battle Must Be Fought in Your Mind

The battles of life are first won and lost in the mind, and exploits are first fashioned in the mind. This means your victories first come from within. You must first believe in yourself, because most of the time, most people will not believe in you. Never stop believing in yourself. Do not accept your present circumstances as an end of your life, and don't believe that your present helpless state is your final destination. Greater things are yet to come.

It is bad enough to allow other people's low opinion of you to affect your progress but even more disastrous when you have a low opinion of yourself. If you do not believe in yourself, no one else will. How you treat or portray yourself will determine how others treat and believe in you.

God's Encounter with Moses

God appeared to Moses and laid out his grand plan for the future of Israel. He had already earmarked Moses to carry out this mission. God was sending him to deliver Israel, and in God's eyes he was the best person equipped to do the job.

Moses was not aware that all that he had been through was to prepare him for this great assignment that would propel him to greatness.

Despite the assurances from God, and the signs he showed him, Moses did not believe in his own ability to lead this mission (Exodus 3: 11; 4: 1,10,13; 6: 12). He had low esteem. He cited being insignificant, that the people would not believe him, that he was not eloquent and fluent in speech, and that he was slow in speech. Moses then responded that God should rather send someone else because he was not qualified.

I believe Moses was not short of confidence at all because as a young man, he stepped in and killed an Egyptian who attacked an Israelite. I feel he was plagued with fear of reprisals should he return to Egypt.

Many of us feel the same way when we are asked to take up a role and feel someone else is more qualified. You may lack the confidence to take up a challenge, but this does not mean you do not have the skillset to accomplish it. If you can develop a positive mindset to tackle it, you would soon find how easy it was. You may be the most suitable candidate, so believe in yourself.

The beauty of God is that he is gracious, and his gifts and calling are without repentance (Romans 11: 29). God will not change his mind about you because you made a mistake. A man will discard you or replace you with someone more gifted. I believe God will also give you another chance despite all the missed opportunities. Do not give up yet.

The Ten Spies

The children of Israel did not believe in their own potential. This was reflected in the responses of the ten spies compared to that of Joshua and Caleb. All twelve spies sent out were not ordinary people; they were tribal leaders. The ten spies had low self-esteem and did not believe in their ability to overcome the inhabitants of Canaan. This lack of confidence was clear in their confession: "But the others said, we can't attack those people; they're way stronger than we are". They spread scary rumours among the people of Israel. They said, "We scouted out the land from one end to the other-it's a land that swallows people whole. Everybody we saw was huge. Why, we even saw the Nephilim giants (the anak giants come from the Nephilim).

Alongside them we felt like grasshoppers. And they looked down on us as if we were grasshoppers" – Numbers 13: 31-33 (The MSG Bible)

This was a defeatist attitude, not a giant-killing mentality, not the mentality of a winner and not the mentality of a people who believe they can overcome obstacles.

Contrast this with the responses of Joshua and Caleb in Numbers 13: 30: "Let's go at once to take the land, we can certainly conquer it". Is it any surprise that even at the age of 85, Caleb still felt he could still conquer lands (Joshua 14: 12). He had a winner's mentality, the spirit of the overcomer, the tenacity of one who would want to succeed at all cost and the perseverance of a person who refuses to be intimidated by any form of obstacle.

The ten spies had a low opinion of themselves, not as victorious children of the living God. They were already defeated in their minds. Here they confess that they are inferior in strength than their enemies even before they engage them in battle. They then state that in their own opinion they looked like grasshoppers. Even worse, they add that the giants also saw them as grasshoppers. How would they know this?

Once they have this mentality, fear takes over, and no amount of convincing will change their minds. The danger is that they then start affecting others with their loser's mentality to the point that the people wept and demanded to return to Egypt (their former poor state; they would rather settle for mediocrity than take a risk).

Many of us have been in situations where we did not have faith in our own ability despite reassurances from people that we could accomplish great things.

Gideon's Encounter with the Angel

When the angel of the Lord appeared to Gideon, he greeted him as a "mighty man of valour and a man with strengths" (Judges 6: 11–24). God sent him on a mission with the statement: "Go in this thy might". This was not how Gideon perceived himself. He did not have faith in his own ability. He perceived himself as insignificant and from an insignificant family. He cites his poor background and his low socioeconomic status as the reason why he was not qualified for the job. God reassures him of his support and protection, but Gideon still asked for a sign so he could believe. God reassures him and helps him accomplish great things. Thank God he was given a chance to fulfil his great potential.

Jeremiah's Calling

When God called Jeremiah (Jeremiah 1: 5), he called him "a prophet to the nations". Jeremiah was not aware of this great future potential. His response (Jeremiah 1: 6) that he did not know how to speak depicted his state of mind. God had to assure him that he had empowered him. You need to believe that God's thoughts and plans for you are for you to excel not to fail.

The examples depicted above suggest that our experiences usually influence our psyches and become a stumbling block to fulfilling our great potential. You can clearly see how easy it is to be affected mentally by your poor background, low socioeconomic status, ethnicity, lack of eloquence, and what you perceive to be your limitations.

I have observed that those with a winner's mentality are not affected by their perceived limitations and would rather improve their strengths whilst working to eliminate or limit the effects of their weaknesses.

You have nothing to lose by thinking big and believing you can excel, because God is on your side. Believe that you can do all things because Christ will strengthen you.

In Isaiah 55: 10–13, God promises us that every word of his concerning us will be fulfilled. I strongly believe God's word and you must too. Use the promises of God and his word of hope to rise to greatness.

Whose Report Will You Believe?

As a young secondary school student, one of my relatives was cutting my hair and commented about the shape of my head and the texture of my hair. In those days I had never visited a barber before because we could not afford it. This lady always commented, "Your head is shaped like a trawler and your hair is not good, it is brittle". As a child I internalised this comment and hated having my hair cut. Most of the time I would sport full grown hair.

However, in my first year at university, a friend was giving me a haircut and accidentally shaved off a large portion, causing an uneven bald spot. We had no choice but to convert it to a close-cut style. The result was excellent. He told me I had a nice round head with underlying curly hair and a round face, so this style was suitable for me. I agreed and believed it because it looked nice. I do not need to tell you that since that year, from 1991 until now, my hair has never grown into an afro again. Persistent negative comments about your ability or inability will in the long term affect you psychologically. Reject those thoughts. Believe in yourself even when others do not. People's negative opinion about you often do not reflect the truth. Negative criticism is subjective and may be borne out of jealousy or a calculated effort to keep you in a low mental state for manipulation. If you believe it and allow it to affect your spirit, it will lead to failure.

In my clinics, I have met many people who suffered mental health issues because someone told this person that his or her significant other no longer felt love and the relationship was over. Some were driven to suicide and others felt their world had fallen apart.

You must understand that someone not loving you does not mean you will never find love anywhere else. One man's meat is another man's poison, and beauty lies in the eyes of the beholder. A breakup can shatter your self-esteem and confidence and make you question yourself, wondering why you are not good for that person. But have you not realised that the person you may be going out with right now may have been someone else's reject? Yet you love that person so much that you see him or her as perfection personified. That should tell you that what one does not treasure, another would kill for. It all depends on perception and values, so know that if you are not valued at one place, another door will open elsewhere. Always use rejection as a stepping stone to becoming better.

Someone's viewpoint is his or her point of view. Opinions will always differ. God in his wisdom created variety.

Believe in God's Report about You

"Though your beginning was insignificant, yet your end will greatly increase" (Job 8: 7 AMP).

Your present circumstances are not a reflection of how your end will be. You must believe this because if you do not, you will place limitations on your potential and ability to excel.

"For I know the plans and thoughts that I have for you, says the Lord, plans for peace and well-being and not for disaster, to give you a future and a hope" (Jeremiah 29: 11 AMP).

How God Sees You Is More Important

"And it came to pass, when they were come, that he looked on Eliab, and said, surely the Lord's anointed is before him. But the Lord said unto Samuel, Look not on his countenance, or on the height of his stature; because I have refused him: for the Lord seeth not as man seeth; for man looketh on the outward appearance, but the Lord looketh at the heart" (1 Samuel 16: 6–7).

In this story, we see how we make judgements on others. When we must pick who we think a talented or gifted person is, or who we feel qualifies to be given a role, our criteria as humans is different from God's criteria. People value status, height, stature, skin colour, qualifications, and a person's connections, for example. God is more interested in your end, or the finished product, not your rugged or difficult beginnings. Your life's journey makes up the sum total of where God is taking you.

Eliab was a strapping young man, tall, handsome, and in the king's army. He appeared qualified. David was possibly uncultured, uneducated, spent most of his time with sheep, and possibly smelt of sheep odour. He would not usually be the kind of guy you would invite to dinner or a posh restaurant. He was raw and possibly lacked table manners, did not dress well, and did not have the stature to fight in the army. He looked disqualified. Eliab's personality and stature almost fooled Samuel, who was a highly respected prophet. Samuel's choice and comment proves how human he was and how even he could make such an error in judgement. If Samuel could make such an error, so can anyone. God proved that it is how he sees us that matters.

That is why when a door of opportunity is shut in your face, do not panic; turn around and knock on another door, and in this second chance, God will shine his face on you.

God's opinion of you is more important than how men see you. People look at outward appearances, but God sees us differently. God sees what a person does not see. He created you and placed in you an innate gift to fulfil a purpose. People only see what they want to see and most times their opinion are wrong anyway. Someone can discourage you by what he or she says to you and that negative comment could destroy your confidence. Sometimes another person's judgement about you may be borne out of his or her own subjective bitter experiences or fears.

Ever spoken to someone who is an eternal pessimist and who has failed at something? The person believes, because he or she has failed, everyone else will fail. But for every failed venture or business, there is someone who succeeds. Anytime people give you an opinion about what they think you cannot accomplish, reflect and align their words or comments with the word of God.

Do not let anyone despise who you are and what you can accomplish. Just because you do not come from a rich family or did not attend a prestigious school or know famous people does not mean you cannot attain your dreams. It is God that lifts one and puts down another. Promotion comes from God (Psalm 75: 6).

You can easily believe what people say about you, that you are not good enough, gifted enough, bright enough, or equipped enough to succeed. Believe in yourself because your present circumstance is not your final destination. Believe what the Bible says about you: "Though thy beginning was small yet thy latter end should greatly increase." – Job 8: 7 (kjv)

The Right Word at the Right Time for the Right Reason

Words are powerful and have an effect, as the Bible suggests (1 Corinthians 14: 10). Receiving correction, rebukes, direction, and instructions are part of life and are needed in every area of life if we are to develop. It is important that when you make a mistake, you become aware of it so that you learn from it and become better. The aim of corrections and rebukes is to build up and edify, not destroy the spirit of a person. The Bible calls it restoring in the spirit of meekness (Galatians 6: 1). It is why I would always prefer to share my problems and issues with a person who can help in my restorative process, not someone who would criticise me in a destructive way. I have no time for such people. No one is perfect, and everyone makes mistakes. No one should sit on a moral high horse and judge others from their own short-sighted view of life. It is important to be told the truth or where you have gone wrong, but it is equally important to understand that the person pointing out your mistakes or faults may not be an enemy. Many people I have spoken to understand they can make mistakes and are open to correction if it is done with love and honesty. The truth is we tend to be more judgemental in our approach.

When you find yourself struggling and need someone to encourage or empower you, do not choose someone who is likely to make you feel worthless or useless. The Bible gives important lessons on the powerful effects of words to the healing of soul and spirit.

Joshua and Caleb Had a Winning Mentality

In Numbers 13: 30, Caleb encourages Israel that despite their clear disadvantages, they were more than able to conquer the Promised Land. Even at the ripe old age of 85, Caleb still had that fiery desire to accomplish greater things (Joshua 14: 10–12).

You are more than able to be victorious despite your clear and obvious weaknesses or disadvantages. Just believe and have faith that the Lord will be with you (Numbers 14: 9).

I see you maintaining your desire to succeed in Jesus's name.

David Had a Winning Mentality

David believed that if God had given him victories in the past over a bear and a lion, then he would also give him victory over Goliath. That faith in God and his word enabled David to accomplish mighty things. You must focus on past victories (1 Samuel 17).

You Need Gracious Words to Break Forth

"Let your speech be always with grace, seasoned with salt, that ye may know how ye ought to answer every man" (Colossians 4: 6).

It means that the words we speak must have the desired outcome of enabling people to be better. The MSG bible puts it this way: "Be gracious in your speech. The goal is to bring out the best in others in a conversation, not put them down, not cut them out" – Col 4:6 (MSG).

Therefore, the main aim of gracious words is to help improve a person. Salt is used to preserve or season food. Therefore, what we say to others who are in crisis must be with the view of preserving and enabling them to rise again.

If you find yourself at a difficult junction of your life right now, find the right person who can speak the right words at the right time for the right reason in your life. Meditate on the following scriptures:

"Like apples of gold in settings of silver, is a word spoken at the right time" (Proverbs 25: 11 AMP).

"A soothing tongue (speaking words that builds up and encourage) is a tree of life, but a pervasive tongue (speaking words that overwhelm and depress) crushes the spirit" (Proverbs 15: 4 AMP).

"A man has joy in giving an appropriate answer, and how good and delightful is a word spoken at the right moment—how good it is!" (Proverbs 15: 23 AMP).

"Pleasant words are like a honeycomb, sweet and delightful to the soul and healing to the body" (Proverbs 16: 24 AMP).

I pray that you will depend on the word of God, which is able to transform your mind and enable you to rise again. May you be empowered and enabled as you break out and break forth in Jesus's name.

Surround Yourself with People with a Winning Mentality

The great Milan teams under Arrigo Sacchi and Fabio Capello produced players who turned out to be good coaches, such as Frank Rijkard, Ruud Gullit, and Carlo Ancelloti. The players that have played under Sir Alex Ferguson won a lot under a manager with a winning mentality. Some of them have gone on to become good managers in their own right: Mark Hughes, Steve Bruce, Ryan Giggs, and Roy Keane come to mind. They have all been tutored by a manager with a winning mentality and grown up in a winning environment. Psychology plays a crucial role in winning—winning teams and a winning positive environment foster a winning mentality.

"He that walketh with wise men shall be wise: but the companion of fools shall be destroyed" – Proverbs 13: 20 (KJV)

In the Christian faith, Archbishop Idahosa, Reverend Enoch Adeboye, Reverend Kenneth Hagin, Kathryn Kullman, Dr Frederick K. C. Price, and Pastor Benny Hinn have all fostered, either directly or indirectly, some of the current great generals in the Christian faith, such as Archbishop Nicholas Duncan Williams, Bishop Dag Heward-Mills, Bishop David Oyedepo, and many others.

Remember that to be able to learn as a mentee, you must see

yourself as naïve and inexperienced and your mentor as wise and discerning. If you can do that, then a lot of wisdom, prudence, knowledge, and discretion will be imparted to you.

Proverbs 1: 5 states: "The wise will hear and increase their learning, and the person of understanding will acquire wise counsel and the skill to steer his course wisely" (AMP).

I pray that the Holy Spirit will grant you a humble spirit. May you be like a child so that you can be nurtured to fulfil your potential.

See Yourself as Victorious and You Will Succeed

Your confessions and utterances reflect the state of your heart or spirit. It depicts your thought processes and how your mind functions. "For as he thinketh in his heart so is he" (Proverbs 23: 7).

What is inside you is what is portrayed on the outside. Jesus said in Matthew 12: 34, "For whatever is in your heart determines what you say" (NLT). Your confessions and what you communicate are related to how you feel about yourself or what you are thinking.

Sometimes people develop this state of mind (defeatist attitude or failing mentality) because of persistent negative statements they have heard uttered about them and the negative perceptions people have of their ability. Over time, they internalise these negative or wrong perceptions about their own ability. You need to develop your inner confidence and self-esteem if you feel you can do more but are restricted by the way your mind works. This inner confidence can be developed. You must slowly remove the wrong information you have internalised through your life and put in more helpful information that will enable you to be bold and courageous. We all try to do the best we can and when we succeed, we are then hailed as successful or geniuses. We always forget how many mistakes successful people have made before getting to the level they have reached.

The danger is not how people see you but how you see yourself— if you see yourself as a grasshopper, then you have the attitude and mentality of a grasshopper. But if you see yourself as a giant slayer, then you will surely find a way to slay giants. When everyone has given up on you, that inner desire to succeed will help you not to give up (1 Samuel 17: 31–40).

Even the wisest of men can make an error in judgement. Remember that Samuel, with all his experience anointing, almost anointed the wrong person to be king if God had not intervened. David did not fit the description of a prospective future king when he was in the bushes looking after sheep, and neither was Joseph when he was in prison. Neither felt sorry for themselves. They held their heads high and kept their hopes alive that one day they would fulfil their dreams.

I pray that you cast away any doubts about your abilities and start believing that God has created you for a purpose. Even when people do not give you the recognition you deserve or appear not to notice that you have anything to offer, continue working to improve yourself. One day God will openly announce you to the world.

David certainly did. Until he slayed Goliath, David was working in Saul's palace, but Saul did not recognise him. He was the cunning harp player who drove demons out with his music, but for some reason Saul did not appear to remember him. It was only after he killed Goliath that Saul took notice (1 Samuel 17: 58).

One day, the same people around you who never took notice will suddenly recognize your greatness. Continue believing that God can do just what he says he will do in your life. Believe in your ability and yourself that you are fearfully and wonderfully made.

A winning mentality must be consciously cultivated, and this is borne out of faith in God's word and in who you are. If you believe that you are uniquely made to accomplish great things, then you will surely accomplish great things.

Everything Is Ready for Your Victory

God is clearly aware that we can easily be afraid, and fear is a limitation to victorious Christian living. In Joshua 1: 2–10, God reveals the plans (Jeremiah 29: 11) he has for the future of Israel. He confirms the extent of his blessings to them and promises that he will not fail or forsake them. You would have thought that having witnessed all the miracles, they would have firmly trusted in God's words. However, fear has always been the oldest human emotion, as was witnessed in the garden of Eden when Adam and Eve fled from the face of God.

Is it any wonder that God sensed the fear in Joshua and reassured and encouraged him to be bold and courageous? It was the only quality he needed to possess what belonged to him and Israel. Three times he reiterates the importance of courage and boldness, even in the face of challenges. God was telling Joshua that there were bound to be challenges ahead, but he had to be strong so those challenges would not overwhelm him (Joshua 1: 9). If you are going to win the battle and break forth, you will need boldness, courage, and resilience. These qualities make up a winning mentality.

You can turn a failure mentality into a winning mentality by changing the way you think. The Bible calls it renewing your mind with the Word of God so that you can think on the right things (Romans 12: 2). Remember that God has not given us a spirit of fear but of power, love, and of a sound mind (2 Timothy 1: 7).

It is my prayer that God takes away any doubts and grants you a winner's mentality. Have faith and you will break out and break forth. Believe in his words concerning your life and start believing in your dream again. You will surely accomplish great things in Jesus's name. Amen.

12

✧

Make God the Centrepiece of Your Life

> Except the Lord build the house, they labour in
> vain that build it: except the Lord keep the city, the
> watchman waketh but in vain.

—Psalm 127: 1

"The horse is prepared for the day of battle, but deliverance and victory belong to the Lord" (Proverbs 21: 31 AMP). It is important for you to know that as you desire to break out and break forth, you need God. This is because without God, your achievements will be insignificant.

Vision without God is simply ambition. Vision has its source from God, but ambition is a human desire. And if your life is all about your ambitions, you will soon discover how empty your life would be without God despite your wealth and all the privileges that wealth can bestow upon you.

A life without Christ is lived in vain and emptiness. Without God you can amass all the wealth in the world, but your soul and spirit will experience emptiness. As you desire to reach the top, understand that being successful and having everything is not the be-all, end-all of life.

People are spiritual beings, and the spirit of humans is not satisfied by physical food—tangible material things. I sincerely believe that material things are only here to make our earthly existence comfortable, but they have a way of taking our attention off the whole duty of people (Ecclesiastes 12: 13). The spirit person finds fulfilment by having a connection with God.

It is why many of us chase material wealth. By the time we have what we want, we are tired, frustrated, empty, sleepless, and disillusioned. Sometimes we attain the dream, become wealthy, and have everything but are riddled with disappointments, bitterness, unforgiveness, and wounds sustained from the battles fought on life's highway. Many of us will do whatever it takes to be rich, famous, have societal status, and rule the world—only to discover at the end of it all that we were chasing after the wind.

Success can be intoxicating, and the wealth, fame, and trappings that success brings can have inherent dangers. I realise that the more you have the more you want. Nothing ever satisfies people.

Ecclesiastes 5: 10 states that, "He that loveth silver shall not be satisfied with silver; nor he that loveth abundance with increase: this is also vanity". For example, when we start our life from the bottom rungs, we cherish the little blessings that come our way. Initially we are excited to own a small used car, rent a small flat, and be able to afford little pleasures. But after a while the car is not big or nice enough, the area you live is not plush enough, and the list goes on and on.

It is why your prayer should be that God grants you grace so that as you break forth, the success will not destroy you (Proverbs 30: 7–9). Without the Lord, life will be very empty at the top because there is a lot of pressure, frustration, and difficult challenges that come along with having wealth and maintaining a wealthy lifestyle. If it were not so, if just being wealthy guaranteed peace, joy, or fulfilment, then some celebrities and famous people would not have committed or contemplated suicide. A considerable number of celebrities and society's elite take drugs, painkillers, abuse alcohol, and abuse many other legal highs to numb the pain of loneliness, emptiness, bitterness, disappointment, abuse, and depression. Your wealth or success should not be your 'strong city', as the Bible says (Proverbs 18: 11).

You need God every step of the way for the following reasons.

For Favour and Mercy

Sometimes, despite your best efforts, you appear to be heading nowhere. It is the Lord that shows mercy and brings favour your way. You will need the favour of God to do well in life (Psalm 5: 12, 102: 13).

You will also need God to stir up the hearts of people to show you favour. It is not a given that because of your gifts or qualifications you deserve a promotion. However, if the Lord is on your side, he will cause doors to open wherever you go (Genesis 39: 21–22; Exodus 3: 21; 1 Samuel 12: 26; Esther 2: 17; Daniel 1: 9).

For the Power to Succeed and Make Wealth

God gives the power and ability to make wealth and the breakthroughs you need comes from him (Deuteronomy 8: 18; Proverbs 12: 1). True and longer lasting success can only be founded on God (Proverbs 8: 18; Matthew 7: 24).

To Nourish Your Spirit

You need the Word of God for nourishment of your spirit, the inner man, as you seek material wealth to bring happiness to your physical self (Proverbs 3: 8)

The more wealth and success you have the more your enemies multiply. His word will nourish and sustain you so you can enjoy "the table he prepares before you" (1 Chronicles 4: 10; Ecclesiastes 5: 19). Long life and good health also come from him (Psalm 91: 16).

To Cope in Times of Crisis

In times of crises, you need the word of God for hope (Psalm 31: 24, 119: 81,114, 147). His word will give you strength in times of adversity and opposition (Psalm 27: 1, 41: 3).

"For you cause my lamp to be lighted and to shine; the Lord my God illumines my darkness. For by You I can crush a troop, and by my God I can leap over a wall (Psalm 18: 28–29 AMP).

"He teacheth my hands to war, so that a bow of steel is broken by mine arms. For thou has girdeth me with strength unto the battle: thou hast subdued under me those that rose up against me" (Psalm 18: 34, 39).

Life is stressful and can wear you down. Sometimes the challenges can be overwhelming and scary. It is the Lord who will teach you how to manage the crises, the Holy Spirit will stand by you, and his word will give you answers to your searching questions in these situations (illuminate your darkness). You will overcome impossible situations because of his word (crush troops, leap over walls, and break steel in your hands). I pray you receive grace if you are going through any challenges.

To Develop Integrity

"Dead flies cause the ointment of the apothecary to send forth a stinking savour: so doth a little folly him that is in reputation for wisdom and honour" (Ecclesiastes 10: 1).

God's word will help you build godly character and moral integrity and will teach you honesty, faithfulness, and patience for long-lasting, successful living. I realise that at the very top, there are so many things that could trip you up and cause you to compromise your integrity, honour, and faithfulness. You need the grace of God to sustain and preserve you.

Build Your House on the Rock

You must build your 'house' (life, wealth, success, career, and all that is important to you) on the rock called Jesus, for our lives depend on him. If you can acknowledge him, believe in him, and serve him with all your heart, mind, and body, then all things are possible.

Life is a winding road with unknown perils and troubles, but we can be certain of God's providence, security, and care if we believe in him. Much as success and wealth is good and must be enjoyed you must also remember that godly wisdom is a better defence because it leads to eternal life (Ecclesiastes 7: 12).

The fear of the Lord is the beginning of wisdom, and this godly wisdom will give you real peace, joy, and contentment.

Develop a Deeper Relationship with God

Your aim must be to develop a deeper relationship with God and go higher in spiritual things. Your main aim is not to be wealthy. It is not a sin to be wealthy because God made certain people wealthy in the Bible, but you will note that they sought God first and the wealth was added as a bonus. They made seeking God the important goal of their life, and in so doing the blessings were added (Matthew 6: 33). Typical examples were Abraham, Isaac, Jacob, and Solomon. Understand that the whole duty of people is to fear God and keep his commandments (Ecclesiastes 12: 13)

You cannot hear and see clearly what the Lord wants you to hear and see about your business, calling, or purpose unless you go higher and deeper with him.

"They that go down to the sea in ships, that do business in great waters; these see the works of the Lord, and his wonders in the deep" (Psalm 107: 23–24).

13

Take The Next Steps: Don't Get Stuck in Your Present State

The Lord our God said to us in Horeb, You have stayed long enough at this mountain. See, the Lord your God has set the Land before you. Go up, take possession land.

—Deuteronomy 1: 6, 21

"A journey of a thousand miles begins with a single step"—Lao Tzu

Spend some time to analyse your life at this moment. Pray to God for divine vision and direction. The next thing you need is to be bold and take the first steps. If it is a business you are hesitating to start, be bold and get it off the ground. Do not be afraid to just trust, believe, and start.

Whatever you want to accomplish, God has already given you the victory. And if God has asked you to do something, it means it is within your ability to accomplish it. You have already been engineered to do well and are programmed to excel.

You Have What it Takes to Succeed

"I returned, and saw under the sun, that the race is not to the swift, nor the battle to the strong, neither yet bread to the wise, nor yet riches to men of understanding, nor yet favour to men of skill" (Ecclesiastes 9: 11).

"There be four things which are little upon the earth, but they are exceeding wise: The ants are a people not strong, yet they prepare their meat in the summer; The conies are but a feeble folk, yet make they their houses in the rocks; The locusts have no king, yet go they forth all of them by bands; The spider taketh hold with her hands, and is in kings' palaces" (Proverbs 30: 24–28).

"There are four small creatures, wisest of the wise they are—ants—frail as they are, get plenty of food in for the winter; marmots—vulnerable as they are, manage to arrange for rock-solid homes; locusts—leaderless insects, yet they strip the field like an army regiment; lizards—easy enough to catch, but they sneak past vigilant palace guards" (Proverbs 30: 24–28 MSG).

The five creatures mentioned in these scriptures appear small, weak, feeble, and disadvantaged in terms of size, power, strength, appearance, and ability to compete for space and resources. All of them have been able to survive in conditions requiring wisdom and operate by wisdom to accomplish near impossible things.

But despite their lack in size, they have survived for centuries by applying wisdom. Come to think of it, dinosaurs are extinct, but all five creatures are still in existence and thriving. Their existence is not yet in much danger and may yet outlive many other creatures. The answer lies in scripture. Wisdom is the principal thing therefore get wisdom (Proverbs 4: 7). It is what you need to break forth.

Ants are small but can lift weights that are heavier than themselves and work through cooperating with each other. They are diligent and disciplined when it comes to gathering food and storing for the winter (saving for hard times). Anthills are intricately constructed edifices. Ants are resourceful creatures, and even when you disrupt them, they quickly regroup and stick to the same routine. When an ant is carrying a load and it falls, it will pick it up and keep trying until it can get the food into the anthill. That is a never-say-die attitude. Ants have been noted to make bridges over water using their own bodies and working as a team. It is diligence in action, keeping at it until the task is accomplished. No job is too small for an ant and no role too menial. It has no reputation or ego. There is no pride that gets in the way of its survival.

Conies (such as marmots, rock badgers, and shephanim) are small creatures indigenous to Africa and the Middle East that have adaptable features which enabled them to live in small spaces in rocks and defend themselves against bigger predators. Not many animals can adapt to living in small rock crevices. This flexibility or adaptability has ensured its survival.

Locusts work together and stick to the same pattern of migration. They respect rank and move in formation with little disruption. Although there is no leader, by depending on each other, they ride the winds and cause a lot of destruction to plantations. Are you able to relate to and work with others to enhance your productivity?

Ants and spiders are always busily working, one building and carrying food, the other weaving web after web to catch prey. Both signify industry and hard work, not laziness, using their 'feeble' attributes to construct webs and anthills of splendour. In a way, the Bible teaches us that by learning from these creatures, we can break forth and become successful, through wisdom, using our God-given gifts.

Lizards and spiders look small, are disregarded, almost ignored when we see them. We fail to notice how versatile, flexible, and adaptable they are, living in palaces many of us can only dream about. I have seen graduates who qualified with a degree but were not humble enough to take up roles other than what they were trained for. That lack of flexibility can stifle your progress. Whilst waiting for that dream job, be wise. There are more poor graduates than less educated millionaires (Ecclesiastes 10: 6–7).

Like the five creatures mentioned in scripture, many of us were not born with a silver spoon in our mouths and are disadvantaged in many ways. Does that mean our life has come to an end? Far from it, because with wisdom we can still fulfil our potential. You must be diligent, disciplined, flexible, and adaptable to break out and break forth.

Many of us lack the diligence and discipline of ants and are also rigid in our thinking and behaviour with no room for change. We love to be in our comfort zone with no disturbance. We are not as flexible, adaptable, or versatile as spiders, conies, and lizards. Ants, spiders, and lizards are so adaptable they can live anywhere and thrive anywhere. Ants can live in bread, small holes, trees, gardens, almost anywhere. You will find a type of spider in almost every continent and any kind of habitation, including the space behind the sideview mirror of my car. Can you live in a village without the comforts of electricity, water, Internet, and other basic amenities if your circumstances called for it?

To progress, you need to be able to adapt to the changing scenes of life. The fact that you qualified as a teacher, an engineer, or a doctor does not mean this is what you must do all your life. At every stage you must be willing to embrace change and be ready to adapt. The future always belongs to those ready for change.

The lesson to be learnt is to not focus on what you think are your weaknesses, frailties, or limitations. All you need is wisdom, so trust God and he will give you wisdom.

Begin Early

Usually, most people who become great achievers start at an early age. But it is still never too late to start something in old age. You can always embrace a new challenge irrespective of your age, as Caleb proved (Joshua 14: 11–12).

There is a great advantage having youthfulness on your side. Young people have energy, fearlessness, and time. They can afford to make certain mistakes because they will have time to learn from the mistakes, correct them and still succeed. As you grow older you become too experienced, too calculating, and less likely to take risks or undertake a new challenge if you have not done so before. It is why, if you have never embarked on a major challenge when you were younger, you should possibly not contemplate it when you are now older. However, irrespective of age, I believe you can always reinvent yourself and accomplish something useful even if you are in your twilight years.

Appreciate the Small Steps You Take Each Time

It is important to work your way to the top in the right way. Small steps lead to big steps and small victories lead to big victories. Do not be discouraged if it appears you are not making any progress because every gradual step brings you closer to fulfilling your vision.

Do not despise the days of small beginnings. Small beginnings are precious foundations that must not be despised. Small steps are vital to the development of anyone who wishes to reach the top and, more importantly, stay there for a long time. Taking small steps is like laying the foundations for a tall building. If the building is going to be tall, the foundation needs to be deep. It takes time to lay such a foundation, but once established, the rest of the building quickly progresses.

Get the basics right, be guided, and slowly build on the foundation of wisdom, and you will surely get there. Do not be in a hurry to reach the top.

Those who are in a hurry to succeed quickly also fall quickly. When you become a millionaire suddenly without having the knowledge and skill to handle and manage money (Ecclesiastes 7: 11–12), you may suddenly become bankrupt. It is why you see a lot of previous great athletes and celebrities go bankrupt despite having earned millions.

You can only manage a business with a thousand-member staff when you have learnt to manage one person over time. You can only manage a £1 million budget when you can effectively invest and manage £1,000.00. Keep trying, keep persevering, and you will get better at what you aim to achieve.

Today you may be the pastor of a small church or leading a small fellowship or even started a small business. Take courage, do not give up, and never despise that opportunity because it is your stage of preparation for greatness. It will just be a matter of time. Appreciate the small steps you must take now. Each little victory gives us an encouragement and belief to achieve even bigger victories. As you overcome each difficult situation you become better equipped to handle the next difficult situation. When you pass the exam in class 1, you are then promoted to class 2 and upwards until you can tackle advanced level exams.

Your beginnings may be small, but I can assure you that your latter end shall be great (Job 8: 7) Do not give up yet. God has a plan for your life. He will order your steps to victory.

"Act now—do not procrastinate, run with your vision" (Habakkuk 2: 1–3).

"If you wait to do everything until you're sure it's right, you'll probably never do much of anything"—Win Borden, American lawyer, businessman, and politician

Procrastination means to defer or delay an action until an opportunity is lost or to put off until another day. Procrastination can affect a person's potential in a significant way. This is because our life goes through seasons, and how well we do in future seasons depends on what you do in the current season.

There are several reasons we all procrastinate. It is interesting to note that I first had a desire to write this book many years ago but started penning the first few pages in August 2008, when the first seeds were sown. I had gone to do a locum at a medical practice but arrived quite early. As I often did, I sat in my car doing my devotion and waiting for the surgery to open. Whilst I read my Bible, I felt a strong urge to write this book as my devotion that day was about strengthening others to accomplish their God-given purpose on earth. It has taken another twelve years to finally complete this book. I kept procrastinating and each time had a competing reason for not completing it.

Many of us keep postponing our vision until it becomes irrelevant. A vision is for an appointment time. There will be many other competing reasons which may be relevant, so we keep postponing developing the gifts that really matter. Many of us keep putting off something we really wanted to accomplish, for example, the skill you wanted to develop, that building project you meant to start, and the course you wanted to take. I believe it is never too late to start anything at any point in our lives if the desire and determination are there.

Spend Time Praying about What You Want to Achieve

"As soon as Zion travailed, she brought forth her children" (Isaiah 66: 8). I will encourage you to pray about your vision because prayer is the fuel that is needed to kickstart your dream. Prayer will be the catalyst needed to get your vision off the ground. As soon as you start committing your vision into God's capable hands, it will start materialising. There is a place for the use of the mind and hard work, but prayer is the key to set loose the bonds of affliction and set you on your way.

Pray That Your Vision Will Not Be Killed Off

Prayer is also needed to ward off enemies away from our set blessings. Satan will place adversaries in your doorway of blessing to block your dreams before they take off. Every great door of blessing that opens to you will have specific adversaries assigned to it by the enemy. If Pharaoh sought to kill baby Moses, and Herod sought to kill baby Jesus, then Satan will seek to kill your vision and gifts in their infancy before they bear fruit. You need to pray the adversaries out the way so you can enter your doors of blessing (1 Corinthians 16: 9).

Pray for Strength to Sustain the Vision

Prayer is also needed to sustain the vision when it takes off. Along the way you will meet many obstacles, and it is your ability to commune with the Lord in your prayer chamber that will ensure that you do not faint along the way. Many dreams and visions have been aborted along the way.

It is only those who wait on the Lord (Isaiah 40: 31) who can renew their strength when the obstacles appear as you progress. You can keep running and walking with strength and not be weary or faint with the challenges you will face.

David always enquired of the Lord when faced with major hurdles, and so must you if do not want to give up. Even the sheer weight of success can destroy you. But God will sustain you if you engage him in prayer.

Pray for Strength because Life's Issues Can Wear You Down

It does not matter how youthful you are or how much zeal you have. Whether you are poor or wealthy, successful or failing, you are not exempt from the pressures of life. You need divine sustenance or success can leave you feeling empty.

"He giveth power to the faint; and to them that have no might he increaseth strength. Even the youths shall faint and be weary, and the young men shall utterly fall. But they that wait upon the Lord shall renew their strength; they shall mount up with wings as eagles; they shall run, and not be weary; and they shall walk, and not faint" (Isaiah 40: 29–31).

Pray for Favour

Sometimes, despite your best efforts, it almost appears as if doors of opportunity are shutting in your face. You must pray for favour every step of the way. Pray for divine and unmerited grace, because this kind of grace ushers you into undeserved blessings.

The Lord showed Joseph mercy and gave him favour in prison. In your most difficult seasons may the Lord show you favour (Genesis 39: 21).

Israel obtained favour in the sight of the Egyptians so much so that there was a wealth transfer. May you also be shown favour. Every place you go, you will not depart the place empty-handed. They will invest in your talents (Exodus 3: 21, 12: 36).

Like Naphtali, may you be satisfied with favour (Deuteronomy 33: 23), and like Samuel, may you have favour with the Lord and with men (1 Samuel 2: 26).

You will have favour before kings and great men as David found favour with Saul and Esther found favour with the king (Esther 2: 17, 5: 2). Daniel also found favour (Daniel 1: 9).

It is my prayer that the Lord causes you to be surrounded by favour on all sides—your businesses, projects, exams, family, and everything you set your hands to do shall be blessed.

A Prayer of Agreement

Father, in Jesus's name, we agree in faith and stand on your word which is true. We pray against any setback spirits, wasteful spirits, barren spirits, or unfruitful spirits in Jesus's name.

We loosen any bonds of affliction and oppression that have shackled us and blocked our visions in Jesus's name. We rebuke any spirit of fear, pride, laziness, distraction, poor attitude, and procrastination.

By the authority of the Holy Spirit, I feel empowered and my talents shall not be wasted. I am filled with a spirit of boldness, sound mind and adventure. My perception is restored, and I can see opportunities that are not obvious.

By the grace of God, I have a good attitude, I can be led and taught and instructed. I receive direction, rebukes, correction, and instruction in all humility with the attitude of a child. I feel blessed, empowered, and ready to take my opportunities in the mighty name of Jesus.

14

A Word of Hope

Then the eyes of the blind shall be opened, and the ears of the deaf shall be unstopped. Then shall the lame man leap as an hart, and the tongue of the dumb sing: for in the wilderness shall waters break out, and streams in the desert. And the parched ground shall become a pool, and the thirsty land springs of water.

—Isaiah 35: 4–7

It Is Never too Late to Start over or Try Again

It is never too late to start again and never too late to dream again. Just look around you. There are so many success stories. It does not matter what your circumstances are; you can still dare to dream again.

Let me walk you through a few achievements that have personally inspired me.

Claudio Ranieri and Leicester City Football Club—a Story of Self-Belief

As a football fan, I followed the English Premier League 2015–16 soccer season with keen interest because of the story of Leicester City football club. Against all odds, they won the premier league title. The story of the team and their manager encouraged me greatly. A team of no-hopers led by Claudio Ranieri, a manager perceived as a failure, defied all odds to win the championship. No one gave them a chance to do what they did. Most of the so-called experts and pundits in the football media wrote them off. The experts based their predictions on the history of both the manager and the team. The team had just escaped relegation and the manager was a laughingstock, and even before a ball had been kicked, they were tipped for relegation. Nobody, including myself, believed they could do what they did.

The manager had fifteen previous managerial jobs and had never won a major league title. He had also been runner-up on a few occasions managing big teams.

When he took over at Leicester City football club, it was his sixteenth management job. He was not given a chance to succeed, and right from the onset the so-called football experts said he would be the first manager to be sacked because he was the wrong appointment. They called him names: tinkerman, nearly-man, dead man walking, and housewife, but he did not react. They said his appointment was uninspiring and a huge gamble. The media mocked him; a few managers made unfortunate remarks about him. One called him 'old and a loser', and one TV pundit said he was a "square peg in a round hole".

The lack of faith in Ranieri's ability stemmed from his past record as a manager: he had only won two major cups (one Italian cup and one Copa del Rey cup) and other smaller cups or titles in thirty years as a manager. The chips were against him and his stock as a manager appeared low. But he had faith in his own ability.

The lowest point of his managerial career was possibly after he was sacked as manager of the Greece national team after they lost at home to soccer minnows Faroe Islands—an unthinkable loss. It appeared as if his career was over. He was sacked by the Greek FA, who said that he was "a most unfortunate choice of coach".

When he took the Leicester job, it could have set him up for his final coup de grace, but he was bold enough to try again soon after he failed with Greece. That boldness, coupled with faith in his own ability, has resulted in the greatest achievement by a team ever in football. Ranieri maintained a dignified silence, trusted his own self-belief, and kept encouraging his team of part-journeymen and part-rejects to keep believing. Week after week they defied the odds and kept chalking one milestone after the other, making history as they went along. The impossible gradually became possible. At every stage of the season, they were doubted—no credit given despite the startling statistics that were clear for all to see.

His achievement turned him into a global name, and his team is known around the world because of their achievement. He has now made history, and a movie may yet be made about the Leicester City soccer story. You never know, a statue may yet be erected in his honour outside the King Power stadium. Not many managers who had previously won championships in the premier league would have statues erected in their honour.

Through all the challenges, Claudio Ranieri remained dignified and graceful and kept believing in himself, his team, and his dream of one day lifting a championship. His attitude and responses in the face of ridicule, frustration, disappointment, and persistent near misses are commendable.

After winning the title, one interviewer asked: "Has it taken you a long time to win a league title?" and his response was, "In my mind I always believe I had to win a title. Every season for me my strength is that I'm a positive man and I believed I could achieve something".

That is an excellent attitude. "For as he thinketh in his heart, so is he" (Proverbs 23: 7).

The Leicester story taught me never to give up even when the chips are down and to always have hope that the future can be bright despite present unfavourable circumstances. Just believe. Sometimes your past may come back to haunt you and your previous bad reputation may seem to follow you. Do not give up on yourself. God is one that always gives a second chance.

Tiger Woods—Resurgence against All Odds

On 14 April 2019 at 6.27 (GMT), I watched live on TV as Tiger Woods knocked the golf ball into the 18th hole to win his fifteenth golf major title at the Masters golf tournament in Augusta, GA. At 43 years old, he had just become the second-oldest winner of the title. It has been described as the greatest comeback in the history of modern sports.

He was awarded the Presidential medal of freedom, one of the highest civilian awards in America, by President Donald Trump. He became the fourth golfer in history to receive this honour. Tiger's redemption was complete.

His last major win was ten years, nine months, and twenty-nine days before his latest victory. Over the past ten years, his image, body, and personal life took a battering, including the collapse of his marriage and his chronic back pain requiring four surgeries. The destruction of his integrity and having to depend on painkillers could have been the end of his career and destroyed his legacy as possibly the greatest golfer in the modern era.

Typically, the media sages had already written him off. Nobody gave him a chance. The media had profited from his victories as well as his demise. Some had already written his sporting epitaph. Woods never gave up his belief that he could win again. He never stopped trying to come back. Ordinary people like you and me may have given up, but what sets greats apart is their will to win. Just as Samson still knew how to battle once his anointing was restored, Woods still knew how to battle once his back would support him.

Tiger Woods said after the victory: "I tried to hang in there. It's an incredible privilege to be awarded the Presidential Medal of Freedom.

Thank you all for your support, and I hope this inspires others to never give up on their dreams". President Trump praised Woods's "relentless will to win, win, win".

But he had been written off, his integrity shattered, image tarnished because of some mistakes he had made. If many of us had gone through the challenges he faced, we may have crumbled and ended our life. Let us also remember that sometimes we do not know the full truth of what someone is going through and the factors that may have led to the mistakes they have made. Yet as humans, we are quick to judge, condemn, and write people off. The good news is that people are not perfect judges; we are not omniscient and can make mistakes. Therefore, learn to ignore some of the comments people may have made about you when you were down. Do not let people's comments be the final nail in your coffin or the last straw to break your back.

Woods proved yet that winners never quit and quitters never win. A winning mentality with resilience will always help an individual bounce back from adversity. Woods persevered. He defied his critics and proved them wrong that he was not finished. He persevered through years of suffering and never gave up until he won his fifteenth major. I believe that even if he does not win another major, he will have proven the point that form is temporary, but class is permanent.

Tiger Wood's comeback in golf taught me a few things: as you take steps to come back from adversity, do not ignore the small victories and achievements you have had in the past. It will boost your confidence. Sometimes you may have to take a few steps backwards as you take a few forwards but do not give up. Keep moving. Maintain your self-belief, and if you've been a winner before, you can win again.

Captain Sir Thomas Moore, NHS Fundraiser: an Inspiration and Beacon of Hope

This great man has given so many people hope during the recent global coronavirus pandemic. Whichever way you look at it, his fundraising effort tells many different stories. He has inspired many people worldwide in many ways. His efforts and achievement tell a story of hope, resilience, and a demonstration that the human spirit can be indomitable.

Who would have thought that it would take a virus pandemic to make him a national hero? At the grand old age of 99, he did something remarkable. It was not a planned dream or vision, just a thought to do something good and remarkable. What he thought was his small contribution to a worthy cause turned out to be the same action that would be his crowning glory, his name etched proudly into the annals of the history of the United Kingdom and at a very difficult period of the world's history.

With a month to his 100th birthday in April, and at the height of a pandemic that was sadly affecting people his age, he decided to raise £1,000 for NHS charities by walking one hundred laps of the 25m (82ft) loop in his garden.

Captain Moore said: "This started as something small ... I didn't ever dream of that sort of money when we started off as a little family joke, to see if we could raise £1,000 and it just went on and on ... I shall be going walking so long as the money comes in for the service, I'll walk, if they contribute, I'll walk".

He raised £32,794,701 from more than one and a half million people from more than one hundred countries.

He told BBC Breakfast: "I did it with pleasure and without any hardship because, as it got on and on, the funds got better and better and it just went on and on. It was absolutely, totally amazing because not only was it in this country but it seemed to go throughout the world". "It seemed to have raised the spirits of so many different countries, which was absolutely amazing and to me it was delightful.

"At no time when we started off with this exercise did, we anticipate we'd get anything near that sort of money ... I am absolutely overwhelmed. Never for one moment could I have imagined I would be awarded with such a great honour by Her Majesty the Queen, the prime minister, and the great British public".

He inspired many others to take to fundraising and show acts of kindness. He brought many to tears with his inspirational words. He demonstrated that no matter how small a vision is, if you are that passionate about it, then you can make it happen.

Captain Sir Thomas Moore began raising funds to thank NHS staff who treated him for a broken hip. His daughter, Hannah Ingram-Moore, told the BBC that the amount raised was "beyond our wildest expectations". When the JustGiving page went live, they thought their £1,000 target was a "real stretch", she said. "He's a stoic Yorkshireman, he's an unruffled straight-down-the-line kind of person and has embraced this adventure as the next stage of his life".

Hannah added: "I believe that life is all about purpose, we all need purpose, and, whilst he's had a life full of purpose, he did fall and break his hip and became much less independent than he had been for the preceding 98 years, and what you have done, the British public, and everyone who's supported him, is giving him his next purpose".

Upon finishing his 100th lap, he gave a message of hope on BBC Breakfast, stating: "At the end of the day we shall all be OK. The sun will shine on you again and the clouds will go away".

She called her father a "beacon of hope in dark times". She said, "I think we all need something like this to believe in and it's for such an amazing cause".

He achieved the impossible within a month, at the age of 100, when many would have given up on life. He raised more than £32 million for a just cause and inspired many to do the same.

For his efforts he got to assist the grand opening of a hospital. He had a Second World War-era Spitfire fly past to mark his 100th birthday. He has now been knighted, and do not bet against it—he may yet get a memorable statue somewhere in the United Kingdom in honour of his efforts.

His story was not only a message of hope but of resilience, belief in dreams, of not giving up even in dark times, and the fact that anything is possible so you should never give up. He could have sat on his sofa unconcerned as the pandemic raged on, justifiably, but did not. He could have sustained a fall resulting in injuries, but it did not deter him. He could have given up after a few attempts as his frail body would surely cause him pain, but he did not. He had a mission and a small vision and an undying passion to do what he felt needed to be done. There were a thousand reasons not to do so, but he overlooked all that and persevered.

Anything is possible, and if it teaches us one lesson, it is that no one should ever give up on themselves at any stage because you never know what could happen to you in life.

Keep Believing

It is not what people say about you that matters. It is not even what opinions people have about you that matter but how much belief you have in yourself. Ultimately, if you are going to break out and break forth, you need to believe that God made you unique and equipped you to do well.

If you can embrace your trials and failures as part of life and as stepping stones to make your life better, then you could learn the lessons from life's difficulties and challenges to your advantage. David trusted the Lord always when faced with different challenges in his life: a lion, a bear, Goliath, the threat of King Saul, rebellion by his own son, and desertion and opposition from trusted men after the incident at Ziklag. Through it all he learnt to trust God.

Many of us will crumble or overact when the tide is against us. There is a lesson to learn from his example in that when things are tough, keep believing even when others have lost faith in your ability to rise. In prison, Joseph kept dreaming and interpreting dreams, in the lion's den Daniel still believed God would show up, and against all odds, David was crowned king.

One of these days someone will call you, and despite your past give you a second chance to make your dream come true. Understand that when one door shuts on your opportunities another will open, and your talents that are of no use to one group will certainly be useful to another. People may not give you a second chance, but understand that God has the final say. He decides who will be promoted and who will not.

The one lesson I have learnt from his experience is to never stop believing in yourself and your dream. It is not over until God calls time on your life. Keep your hopes alive. Have faith in God and trust him to help you break out and break forth. Your life is about to begin, and the best is yet to come despite your present circumstances. The best days of your life are still in front of you.

Isaiah 43: 18–19 encourages us to put the past behind us and look ahead with hope because the Lord is on our side: "Do not remember the former things, or ponder the things of the past. Listen carefully, I am about to do a new thing, now it will spring forth; Will you not be aware of it? I will even put a road in the wilderness, rivers in the desert" (AMP).

A Small Beginning Does Not Mean a Small Ending

The Bible states that we are fearfully and wonderfully made and assures us that though our beginnings are small (humble), our latter end shall be greater. In all things we get encouraged that we are more than conquerors. There are so many inspiring stories that encourage us to not give up on ourselves even when the odds seem against us.

Against all odds, Abraham and Sarah conceived, Hannah bore Samuel, Esther became queen, David became king, Jephthah became a judge, and Ruth married Boaz and became the great-grandmother of Jesus. Despite being older than 80, Moses performed or witnessed miracles in Egypt: parting the Red Sea, manna falling from heaven, water gushing from the rock at the strike of a rod, and speaking to God face to face. Your best is yet to come. Many of these stories encourage us to be hopeful.

I have just fulfilled a dream of writing a book. If I do not write another book, at least I have managed to complete something I desired to do. I was not a writer or author but after all these years I have still managed it. Now I call myself a writer.

I want you to believe that whatever desire and dreams you have can be accomplished if you set your heart to it. Since you are reading this book, know that it was one of my long-cherished dreams to write a book that inspires people not to give up on their dreams. You can accomplish something.

Dreams may start exceedingly small, but with desire, vision, ambition, passion, and commitment, that dream may become big. You are certainly not worthless. In the hands of God, little can become much, clay can be turned into beautiful pottery, and a life that looks like a wasteland can be made fruitful again.

Dare to dream, and you can hopefully one day inspire others. Everyone has something to offer, and collectively we can make the world a better place.

The journey may be tough, the road may look rough, but if you don't give up on that vision, one day it will come to pass. Joseph dreamt and it happened because he believed it and had faith. His journey involved being thrown into a pit, being sold as a slave, being accused of a crime he had not committed, and finally spending time in jail. Little did he know that everything that had happened to him was part and parcel of his journey to greatness.

What you have been through so far and are going through now, God will use those experiences as stepping stones to greatness. All those experiences work together as a package for us. What I mean is that all that you have experienced up until now—the good, the bad, and the ugly experiences are meant for a reason.

The Lord Will Restore Your Wasted Years and Establish You

Out of what you thought was failure will come a blessing. Impossible things are always possible with God. What you do not think can happen will suddenly become possible. If God raises the dead, he can breathe life in your current situation if you believe. I pray you experience the supernatural hand of God in your life.

"And I will restore to you the years that the locust hath eaten, the cankerworm, and the caterpillar, and the palmerworm, my great army which I sent among you. And ye shall eat in plenty, and be satisfied, and praise the name of the Lord your God, that hath dealt wondrously with you: and my people shall never be ashamed" (Joel 2: 25–26).

"I will open rivers in high places, and fountains in the midst of the valleys: I will make the wilderness a pool of water, and the dry land springs of water. I will plant in the wilderness the cedar, the shittah tree, and the myrtle, and the oil tree; I will set in the desert the fir tree, and the pine, and the box tree together" (Isaiah 41: 18–19).

I see your fallow grounds being tilled, your wasted gifts being restored, every shattered dream resurrected, and any dry life being refreshed. The Lord shall make you productive again, hopelessness is giving way to hope, and help is coming to you if you feel helpless. The Lord will make a way when there seems to be no way.

You will be able to dream again because God is granting you perception. Your ears will be open to counsel as God raises good mentors for you. Any dumb spirit will be overcome, and many shall hear about you in many nations. You will be energised like a deer, strength is coming back into your body and you will rise and run with your vision like a hart running with excitement.

If your life feels like a parched desert or wilderness, take heart because you will break out and break forth to be a blessing to many. I see God lifting you up to higher heights in Jesus's name.

A Special Prayer for You

I declare that the heavens shall open, and a blessing shall be poured upon your life. Let there be a divine turn around. As you trust in the Lord and place your faith in him, you shall be like a tree planted by the rivers of water. You will succeed at the right season of your life. May you receive the latter rain even the former rain upon your life. The Lord will grant you unmerited favour and let every kind of grace abound to you. He will fulfil his Word in your life in Jesus's name.

Afterword

Your Whole Duty to God

It is not how much we have, but how much we enjoy, that makes happiness.

—Charles Spurgeon, English Particular Baptist preacher

Success Means Different Things to Different People

"And ye shall serve the Lord your God, and he shall bless thy bread, and thy water" (Exodus 23: 25).

Let me sound a word of caution as I end this book. As a child of God, he will bless you as you serve him, but with that blessing comes the dangers of wealth.

It is absolutely a good thing to want to do well in life. It is neither a crime to want to fulfil your potential nor a bad thing to want to be rich. It is the danger of pursuing riches and becoming wealthy at all cost which has, arguably, fuelled the downfall of many.

In your pursuit of wanting to do well, pause briefly and ponder the following questions:

- What is my motive for wanting to be successful in life?
- What is driving me to want to be rich or wealthy at all cost?
- Am I striving to be successful to impress others and boast?
- Is my desire to fulfil my potential the purpose for which God created me?

The pursuit of happiness by all of us is obvious for all to see. We believe that life is great when we are successful, wealthy, and healthy.

God wants us to be healthy, happy, and prosperous but in a holistic way. "Beloved, I pray that in every way you may succeed and prosper and be in good health (physically), just as (I know) your soul prospers (spiritually)" (3 John 1: 2 AMP).

Money Is Useful but Not the Be-All and End-All in Life

For many people, including Christians, the desire to do well is to become wealthy and raise our social status.

Money is important but not the most important thing in life. It is essential but not the ultimate resource needed to be happy. Being wealthy is not necessarily indicative of a successful and fulfilled life.

How many houses can you live in at the same time? How big a space does one need to live comfortably? How many cars can you drive at a time? How much space on the bed do you need to have a good night's sleep? How many toilets do you need to sit on daily to have a good bowel movement?

A person wakes up at dawn, goes to work, expends all his or her energy in the pursuit of 'the dream', comes home exhausted, and repeats the same cycle for the rest of his life. And then we get tired chasing the dream and leave it all behind and depart into eternity. For many, this 'chasing after the wind' leads to disillusion, loss of hope, disinterest, and sometimes suicide from helplessness. There must be meaning to life, surely a purpose to our existence. That purpose, dear reader, can be found by having a personal relationship with God.

As you desire to have more and more, consider why you are so desperate before it leads to your destruction.

The peace in people's homes have been shattered because of money, destroyed marriages, wrecked homes, lost friendships, broken relationships, and lost lives in pursuit of wealth. Think carefully before your desires lead you to destruction and shatters your peace.

Money Answers Some but Not All of Life's Questions

"For wisdom is a defence, and money is a defence: but the excellency of knowledge is, that wisdom giveth life to them that have it" (Ecclesiastes 7: 12).

"A feast is made for laughter, and wine maketh merry: but money answereth all things" (Ecclesiastes 10: 19).

When something is described as a defence, it means it can protect you from harm or resist an attack. In a way, money protects us against the effects of poverty.

You can afford many things if you have money. It can defend you against the evils of poverty. You can afford decent housing and clothing, and a better education for your children and yourself. When you are ill, you can pay for good medical care at the right time if you have money saving you from untimely death. You can even afford to go on a foreign holiday if you have money. In a way, because money helps us accomplish many things, it becomes a defence for many.

But money is not the source and key to happiness but may bring some happiness because it will provide relief. What will sustain you is not necessarily money but wisdom that comes from the knowledge and fear of God. What brings real happiness and joy is a connection with God.

It Is Foolishness to Work so Hard Just to Be Rich

The wisest man that ever lived, King Solomon, said, after careful observation, in Ecclesiastes 1: 2, "'Vanity of vanities', says the preacher.

'Vanity of vanities! All (that is done without God's guidance) is futile, meaningless—a wisp of smoke, a vapor that vanishes, merely chasing the wind)'" (AMP).

Our life and existence on earth is so short and must be enjoyed. Work is important, good for the body, and even great for the mind. You must have ambition and a desire to do well. But your ambition must not to be rich at all costs. Do not put yourself through so much stress just to be rich. That is not a good ambition. It has inherent dangers. Not everyone can handle wealth, and not everyone can manage riches and maintain their sanity. It takes wisdom to understand this.

"Do not weary yourself (with overwhelming desire) to gain wealth; cease from your own understanding of it. When you set your eyes on wealth, it is suddenly gone. For wealth certainly makes itself wings, like an eagle that flies to the heavens" (Proverbs 23: 4–5 AMP)"

Try to understand that the most valuable things on earth that bring happiness, laughter, and joy are free. Knowing and loving God is free, your salvation is free, sharing and having good relationships with family is free, and dwelling with your neighbours in peace and love is also free.

Make every effort not to kill yourself with evil ambition.

A Carnal Desire for Riches Is a Snare

"He who loves money will not be satisfied with money, nor he who loves abundance with its gain. This too is vanity (emptiness). When goods increase, those who consume them increase. So what advantage is there to their owners except they see them with their eyes. The sleep of a working man is sweet, whether he eats little or much; but the full stomach (greed) of the rich (who hungers for even more) will not let him sleep" (Ecclesiastes 5: 10–12 AMP).

I have stopped being amazed by how human greed can cause some people to embezzle money. Corrupt officials can steal millions, even billions whilst their fellow citizens die from poverty, joblessness, diseases, and hunger. I used to wonder whether they are so wicked and their conscience so seared that they have no compassion. Many cannot live peacefully and happily with their stolen wealth and would go to great lengths to hide it. But from the scripture above, I can understand why. Enough is never enough once a man smells the sweet scent of money; he would do whatever it takes to have more and more.

"Hell and destruction are never full; so the eyes of man are never satisfied" Proverbs 27: 20).

We are all never satisfied with what we have. We can always justify why we need more. We want more money, more cars, and more power. I remember when I bought my very first car, a used car, called 'brand-new second-hand' in my country. It was reasonably old but, in my eyes, it was like a little gem. Like many new things we acquire, I treasured it, washed it each week, and loved the car. Within a year, my earnings had increased and suddenly this car that had served me so well looked old, not fit for purpose anymore, not befitting my status as a medical practitioner. I had moved up, so my acquired tastes had changed. It did not take long to replace this car with a better one.

For many of us, this is what life has become. We strive and stress so much for more money and plunge ourselves into debt just to spend on things that never satisfy. Make every effort not to fall for the snare of just pursuing riches as it can be deceitful.

Reasons People Seek to be Successful and Wealthy

Most people seek to do well so they can live and not just survive. They want to make ends meet as the monthly wages or allowances cannot be stretched far enough to meet all our monthly commitments. We want better jobs and better wages so we can afford the nice things in life. That is genuine and a basic human right. However, like a predator smelling the blood of its prey, once we have sniffed that sweet smell of success, it starts a chain reaction that never stops.

There are other reasons why some would want to be rich.

The Pride of Life (1 John 2: 15–17)

Some of us are striving so we can boast about what we have and show off. This had driven many to steal, kill, lie, and pretend. It creates an appearance of being successful (borrowed glory). It is like a facade but inside our homes we are hurting, crippled by debts, loans, and contracts we cannot fulfil. But pride always comes before a fall and soon we are so crippled with debts that we become depressed. Once you start loving material things, there is no stopping because the eyes are never satisfied.

To Spend on the Pleasures of Life (Luke 8: 14)

Who does not want to have fun-filled holidays and all the pleasurable things life can offer? It becomes a dream, an obsession, especially when we see the rich and famous paraded by the media. They become our role models, and we yearn to look and be like them. But happiness is not found in these things.

Pure Greed and Lust for Riches (James 1: 14–15)

Some people are plain greedy, and this greed fuels their insatiable desire for more. The destruction of some people has come about because they did not know when to stop.

To Compare Ourselves to Others (2 Corinthians 10: 12)

In a world where society has been divided into classes and status has become so important, everyone wants to be seen in an A-list category. Young men and women would sell drugs and commit crimes so they can be like the other kids living in the estate portraying wealth. It is not wisdom

A Quality, Fulfilled Life Has Nothing to Do with Material Things

Being fulfilled has nothing to do with being rich; real joy and happiness is a spiritual experience. Luke 12: 15 states, "And he said unto them, Take heed, and beware of covetousness: for a man's life consisteth not in the abundance of the things which he possesseth".

God gives the ability to make true riches and wealth (Deuteronomy 8: 18; 1 Chronicles 29: 11–12) and the power to enjoy it (Ecclesiastes 5: 19).

Wealth can make you proud and forget your humble beginnings. Many have suddenly stopped believing that God exists when they have become successful. Success has a way of making us lose the quality of humility and humanness that we possessed when we did not have much (Deuteronomy 8: 11–14; Proverbs 30: 8–9).

Wealth Can Destroy Your Peace and Happiness

It is obvious from scripture that if your main reason for success is to be rich, you can destroy your life in the process.

"But they that will be rich fall into temptation and a snare, and into many foolish and hurtful lusts, which drown men in destruction and perdition. For the love of money is the root of all evil: which while some coveted after, they have erred from the faith, and pierced themselves through with many sorrows" (1 Timothy 6: 9–10).

You Must Guard Your Heart and Your Desires

Your desire to break forth must not be to be rich or wealthy at all cost. It must rather be a desire to fulfil your God given potential and be a blessing to humankind. In a matter of time the riches may naturally follow. Money must be a means to an end and not the end of your life. What is the point of being blessed with wealth that leads to your destruction? Will it be profitable gaining the whole world and losing your very soul to hell? (Mark 8: 36) Certainly not. Be careful what you wish for because not all that glitters is gold, and the grass is not always greener on the other side.

Would I buy a Ferrari for an irresponsible, reckless 17-year-old who just passed his driving licence? No, because I would just have signed his death warrant. He would crash the car and, in the process, end his life. Therefore, many of us may desire riches, but God may keep it away from us to preserve us. God, who is better than a parent, knows the desires of our heart and the real motive or reasons we want to succeed. If you commit your life to him, he will guide and direct you.

"Keep thy heart with all diligence; for out of it are the issues of life" (Proverbs 4: 23).

Learn to Be Content; It's a Spiritual Quality

"But godliness with contentment is great gain and having food and raiment let us be therewith content" 1 Timothy 6: 6, 8).

Being content at all stages of your life is a spiritual quality, you cannot have everything in life. Without contentment you will not value what you have and would not appreciate the blessings you have. Remember that people pretend, so it is dangerous to want to be like someone else who appears successful. There is a price to pay for success, and you may not be equipped with what it takes to handle wealth.

It is important to always remember that you do not need much to make you happy. Happiness is a state of mind, and, does not come because of what you have but in being content with what you have and valuing things like family, friends, and the community around you.

"Better to have little, with fear for the Lord, than to have great treasure and inner turmoil. A bowl of vegetables with someone you love is better than steak with someone you hate" (Proverbs 15: 16–17 NLT).

"Better a dry crust eaten in peace than a house filled with feasting and conflict" Proverbs 17: 1 NLT),

"And yet, better to have one handful with quietness than two handfuls with hard work and chasing the wind" (Ecclesiastes 4: 6 NLT).

You can still be content and happy as the scriptures above show. It is a mindset you must cultivate. Life is simple, but many of us love complexities. Living with just a little or a handful requires resilience. Trying to resist peer pressure and the pride of life, the lust for many things, and the deceitfulness of riches is no mean feat. You need mental fortitude and faith to trust in God.

"But if your trust is in the Lord, he will direct your path. 'Commit your works to the Lord (submit and trust them to him), and your plans will succeed (if you respond to his will and guidance)" (Proverbs 16: 3 AMP).

First Seek to Know God and His righteousness.

There are several people in the Bible that God blessed including Abraham, Isaac, Jacob, Joseph, and Solomon. They did not make it their sole purpose to get rich but in their pursuit of knowing and loving God, physical wealth was given to them.

Life can wear you down, the pursuit of success and the desire for riches and material things has destroyed many. Man is engineered for success and ordained to be fruitful. There are no limits to our potential. But trying to live life without Christ and without knowing God, is utter foolishness. You will eventually be worn down by the sheer weight and pressure of life if Christ is not in it. Draw closer to God and desire to know him more (Jeremiah 9: 23–24).

Understand That Jesus Is the Bread of Life Who Satisfies and Sustains

As we become successful, we get to the point where life feels empty despite all we seem to have achieved and possess. The journey can wear you down, and living in this evil world can make you depressed. We all seek happiness, and we seek things that will plug the emptiness, fill us with peace and joy and make us feel fulfilled. But all the things we seek, chase, kill for, and strive for never fill the vacuum in our spirit.

There is a void in people that cannot be filled with material things and achievements. That void can only be satisfied when we encounter the Lord Jesus Christ. He is the answer.

"And gavest them bread from heaven for their hunger, and broughtest forth water for them out of the rock for their thirst" (Nehemiah 9: 15).

> Then Jesus said unto them, Verily, verily, I say unto you, Moses gave you not that bread from heaven; but my Father giveth you the true bread from heaven. For the bread of God is he which cometh down from heaven, and giveth life unto the world. Then said they unto him, Lord, evermore give us this bread. And Jesus said unto them, I am the bread of life: he that cometh to me shall never hunger; and he that believeth on me shall never thirst. (John 6: 32–35)

Jesus is the only one who can offer the living water that will bring contentment, take away greed and covetousness, and bring fulfilment. This bread of life and living water prevents us from thirsting after material things that are useless, baseless, corruptible, and insatiable. Jesus Christ is the answer to the happiness you are looking for.

God Is Working behind the Scenes for You

God will not leave you to struggle. He will lead you and help you overcome all the challenges and obstacles that come your way. Learn to trust in God despite your present circumstances. Learn to believe in him and allow him to lead you. He has good plans for you which are designed to end well (Jeremiah 29: 11).

The Lord is merciful and gracious, and his promises are true. The fact you are not dead from all your past challenges and failures means he has been preserving and carrying you through the storms of life. The waters and rivers of life will not drown you, and those fiery challenges will come but will not burn you up. His grace is always sufficient. May you receive help from the Lord if you are going through challenges right now.

"And the Lord, he it is that doth go before thee; he will be with thee, he will not fail thee, neither forsake thee: fear not, neither be dismayed" (Deuteronomy 31: 8).

"When thou passest through the waters, I will be with thee; and through the rivers, they shall not overflow thee: when thou walkest through the fire, thou shalt not be burned; neither shall the flame kindle upon thee" (Isaiah 43: 2).

"For the mountains shall depart, and the hills be removed; but my kindness shall not depart from thee, neither shall the covenant of my peace be removed, saith the Lord that hath mercy on thee" (Isaiah 54: 10).

Choose to Trust in God and Live for Him

"Trust in the Lord with all thine heart; and lean not unto thine own understanding. In all thy ways acknowledge him, and he shall direct thy paths" (Proverbs 3: 5–6).

It is important to understand that people do not exist in a vacuum, and that people are spirits with souls that live in a physical body. People make their own plans and how they want to live. When you are wise, you learn to depend on God to direct your life. Do not put your trust in money and material things (Isaiah 31: 1; Jeremiah 17: 5–8).

As you make your plans, commit them to the Lord, and he only will bring you to the perfect end (Proverbs 16: 1–3). He knows your heart, your motives, your thoughts, and your goals. He will establish your thoughts, give you the right answers, and patiently guide you to the perfect end. Focus on the Lord, and he will bring you to a great and fruitful place. He has promised and will not fail.

Ponder over the words of the great King David to his son, Solomon, when he was dying. He summed up the steps to true riches and greatness in this scripture: "And thou, Solomon my son, know thou the God of thy father, and serve him with a perfect heart and with a willing mind: for the Lord searcheth all hearts, and understandeth all the imaginations of the thoughts: if thou seek him, he will be found of thee; but if thou forsake him, he will cast thee off for ever" (1 Chronicles 28: 9).

Solomon aptly summed up the 'whole duty of man', which is to love God and serve him.

"Let us hear the conclusion of the whole matter: Fear God, and keep his commandments: for this is the whole duty of man" Ecclesiastes 12: 13).

The Shema Yisrael Prayer—Declaration of Faith and Prayer

"Hear O Israel: The Lord our God is one Lord: And thou shalt love the Lord thy God with all thine heart, and with all thy soul, and with all thy might" (Deuteronomy 6: 4–5).

I believe that if your whole purpose is to know the one true God, love him, serve him, and live for him with all your heart, then you will have good success and enjoy this success in peace, love, and safety.

Pray This prayer for Your Future

Dear Lord, may I not be the same again. Turn my life around. Let me draw closer to you, let me have a divine encounter with you. Let my barren life be fruitful, and let my thirsty soul be filled with your living waters. Revive my spirit and stir me up to good works.

Holy Spirit, be my guide, lead me to the Father and draw me closer to Jesus Christ. Be my Teacher, my Revelation, and my Comforter in times of difficulty. Strengthen me in my inner man so I can walk this walk of faith. Thank you, Lord Jesus, for your grace and abounding mercies. In Jesus's precious name. Amen.

Resources

- www.thedictionary.com.
- www.dictionary.cambridge.org.
- www.businessdictionary.com.
- www.coachingnetwork.org.uk.
- Advanced English Dictionary and Thesaurus.
- The Gill Bible Commentary.
- Merriam-Webster Dictionary.

'Please send any reviews, comments, contributions or invitations to: info@robcann.org.uk – thank you'

Printed in the United States
By Bookmasters